revitalize
your
spiritual life

revitalize
your
spiritual life

A WOMAN'S GUIDE for
VIBRANT CHRISTIAN LIVING

THOMAS NELSON
Since 1798

NASHVILLE   DALLAS   MEXICO CITY   RIO DE JANEIRO

Revitalize Your Spiritual Life
© 2010 by Thomas Nelson, Inc.

Published in Nashville, Tennessee, by Thomas Nelson. Thomas Nelson is a registered trademark of Thomas Nelson, Inc.

Thomas Nelson, Inc., titles may be purchased in bulk for educational, business, fund-raising, or sales promotional use. For information, please e-mail SpecialMarkets@ ThomasNelson.com.

Scripture references are taken from the following sources:

The King James Version of the Bible (KJV). Public domain. *The Message* (MSG) by Eugene H. Peterson. © 1993, 1994, 1995, 1996, 2000. Used by permission of NavPress Publishing Group. All rights reserved. The NEW AMERICAN STANDARD BIBLE® (NASB), © The Lockman Foundation 1960, 1962, 1963, 1968, 1971, 1972, 1973, 1975, 1977, 1995. Used by permission. The New Century Version® (NCV). © 2005 by Thomas Nelson, Inc. Used by permission. All rights reserved. The Holy Bible: New International Version® (NIV). © 1973, 1978, 1984 by International Bible Society. Used by permission of Zondervan Publishing House. All rights reserved. The New King James Version (NKJV). © 1982 by Thomas Nelson, Inc. Used by permission. All rights reserved. The Holy Bible, New Living Translation (NLT). © 1996, 2004. Used by permission of Tyndale House Publishers, Inc., Carol Stream, Illinois 60189. All rights reserved. The New Revised Standard Version of the Bible (NRSV). © 1989 by the Division of Christian Education of the National Council of the Churches of Christ in the U.S.A. All rights reserved. J. B. Phillips: The New Testament in Modern English Revised Edition (PHILLIPS). © J. B. Phillips 1958, 1960, 1972. Used by permission of Macmillan Publishing Co., Inc.

Selections were previously published in individual titles by the following authors: Jill Briscoe, Jill Hubbard, Tammy Maltby, Marilyn Meberg, Stormie Omartian, Paula Rinehart, Angela Thomas, Sheila Walsh, Lisa Whittle. Selections have been edited from the originals.

Library of Congress Cataloging-in-Publication Data available

ISBN 978-1-4002-0279-9

Printed in the United States of America

10 11 12 13 14 WC 6 5 4 3 2 1

Contents

Introduction:
Finding Our Way Again

When We've Lost Our Way

Angela Thomas (*When Wallflowers Dance*)

Waking up to your life is a process.

    I was thirty-eight. A grown woman with half a lifetime of experiences. Fairly educated and organized. But I couldn't choose between blueberries or strawberries for dessert at a friend's dinner party. We laughed off my indecision, and I sat at the table watching my girlfriend serve me a little of both, wondering, *Why did that just cause me stress? Why don't I know what I like?* My silly quandary over dessert was just the beginning of a question that went home with me. In the next weeks, I kept turning those thoughts over and over in my mind. Eventually the deeper questions began to surface. *What kind of a woman is thirty-eight years old and doesn't know what she wants for dessert? Why don't I care about little things? Where did I go?*

Why don't I feel anything anymore? Why don't I enjoy anything? When did I stop becoming?

It wasn't just that I couldn't make a decision about dessert; I began to realize that I really didn't know anything about me at all. I had no preferences. No top fives. No particular likes or dislikes. I had no idea what kind of music I liked to listen to, so mostly I listened to nothing. I couldn't tell you what my favorite restaurant was or if I'd like to go to the mountains or the beach for vacation. I couldn't choose a paint color with any confidence that I'd like it next week. I collected nothing for fear of collecting something I'd hate later. I realized I always chose what I thought would make someone else happy. About fifteen years of doing that and there was no me left.

I hadn't always been so uncommitted and uninteresting. I literally wore out an eight-track because I loved the funky music of Earth, Wind & Fire in high school. I was adamant about wanting yellow shag carpeting with daisy light fixtures in my bedroom. Mama's fried cube steak was my favorite food, and cherry pie was my favorite dessert. I read everything Lois Lenski ever wrote. I wanted to be the best varsity cheerleader in our county. I loved waking up and I loved Jesus and my youth group and a cherry cola called Cheerwine. I remember laughing a lot back then. And I remember the Angela I was discovering inside me.

College and seminary were vibrant years that I can play back in my head in Technicolor. The world was alive to me. God was my passion. I could see and touch and feel. It seems I danced a lot back then. And told jokes. And trusted God. Still excited and still hoping.

But about four years ago, I was a grown woman in a daze. I kind of knew I was dead to life because I could see other people living out there somewhere, but I didn't believe I could ever be alive again. Actually, I'm not sure I even wanted a real life with real passion. I had become the un-person. Neutral. Safe. Asleep. Numb. Vanilla. Harmless. With an un-life. Going through the motions. Surviving. Reacting. Smiling. Somewhere along the way, I had given up. I guess somewhere along the way, it seemed the easiest thing to do.

Most of us don't just wake up one morning and think to our-selves, *I am officially giving up on life. I am checking out. Numbing down. Going nowhere. Only breathing and surviving from here on out.* But for many of us it happens anyway. Various degrees of giving up. Various degrees of an un-person with an un-life.

I have tried to retrace my steps to figure out what happened to the woman I was becoming all those years ago. I have a firstborn, pleaser personality. At some point, I realized that I got a lot of energy from making everyone else happy. So keeping people happy eventually became more important than knowing my purpose or becoming anything.

As a mom, having four children in seven years took its toll on my heart. I thought I could be the most amazing mother on the planet, but it turns out that survival was about the best I could do. They were clean and fed, but my soul fell fast asleep in those baby years. I didn't mean for it to happen. I tried to pretend it didn't, but a little of me died in the ten years of diapers.

I was married fourteen years. The divorce was embarrassing.

In all those years my heart grew numb in order to cope. More of me was gone. Add up the years and the events. My ridiculous need to please. The people and the pain. The weariness of an overwhelming life. Take away the community that comes from honesty. Take away the spiritual nourishment that could have come from being known and understood. Add the pride of a woman who refuses to own her flaws or admit to her wounds. Stir in fear. Worry. Doubt. Insecurity. The lies we come to believe. Subtract vulnerability. Heap on pretending. There you have the woman I was becoming.

The un-woman just trying to blend in. Giving up a little more every day. The one who couldn't even choose between berries. A woman just watching the world go by. Afraid. Without confidence. A wallflower.

A while ago I had a very specific conversation with a woman. Her children were grown. The house was clean enough. She had the whole rest of her life to live. "What do you love?" I asked. "What are your passions? If you could dream big or become anything, what would it be? Let's pray together, hear from God, get a plan, and work the plan." She was enthusiastic and at the time seemed motivated to go forward. We talked about it a few more times over the next months. At least three years have gone by since our first conversation. The kids are a little older. The house is a little cleaner. She has prayed and prayed. Nothing has changed in her life or in her purpose. Wallflower is a safe place, and she is choosing to stay there. I think she's afraid of becoming.

I know what it feels like to be afraid. As many options as there are for fear, it seems one or many can get into my head and paralyze my heart. And when my heart is seized with fear, then I stand still or pull inside my emptiness to mourn. Then life goes by without me. And years go by without any significant growth or change.

Even worse, time can go by and a woman can emotionally begin to fade away. Barely noticeable at first. Only a little giving in to fear at a time. And then one day, the woman who has lived gripped by fear has watched it all pass by. There are no days left. She missed her purpose. Fear won, and the wallflower is all she's become.

She is just one of us. We're over it on the inside. Life holds no fascination. Adventure sounds exhausting. Friendships aren't worth it. We're tired, and we want to be left alone. Being a wallflower sounds like that long nap we've been needing.

> Are you tired? I imagine that you are because everyone I know is exhausted.
>
> Are you disappointed, depressed, or even worse, hopeless? You are not alone.
>
> Have your dreams all died or maybe you have failed in their pursuit?
>
> Have you become afraid of everything or a lot of things?

I hear you and some days I'm with you, but you cannot give up. Evidently, you woke up this morning still breathing. And every day you are left on this earth is a day that God intended for your life to matter. Not only does your life matter, I do not believe that God means for any of us to live an un-person, un-life, wallflower existence. I believe he meant for us to dance.

Why Even Good Christian Girls Need a Word of Grace

Tammy Maltby (*Confessions of a Good Christian Girl*)

A story is told of a carefree young girl who lived at the edge of a forest, where she loved to play and explore and take long, adventurous journeys. But one day she journeyed too deep into the forest and got lost. Evening approached, and as the shadows lengthened, the girl grew worried.

She tried one path after another, but none looked familiar. And none led her home.

Deeper and deeper into the forest the frightened girl ran. Her skin was scratched from limbs whipping her as she pushed her way through the overgrowth. Her knees were scraped from tripping in the dark. Her face was streaked from her tears. She called for her parents, but the forest seemed to swallow her words. After hours of trying to find her way home, the exhausted child came to a clearing in the forest, where she curled up on a big rock and fell asleep.

Meanwhile, the girl's parents were frantic with worry. They searched the forest for her, cupping their hands and calling her name. But there was no answer. As night fell, the parents' search grew more intense. They enlisted the help of friends and neighbors. They even asked strangers from town to help them search for their lost little girl. Over the course of the night, many of the searchers went home.

But not the girl's father. He kept on combing the woods, even when his wife left to tend to their other children. He searched all night and on into the next morning. Finally, at the first light of dawn, he spotted his daughter asleep on the rock in the middle of the clearing. He ran as fast as his legs would take him, calling her name.

The noise startled the girl awake. She rubbed her eyes. Then, reaching out to him, she caught his embrace.

"Daddy!" she exclaimed. "I found you!"[1]

It's a beautiful story. A familiar story. And if you've been a Christian for any time at all, you probably guessed the punch line.

Yes, I'm that lost little girl.

The thought of it still produces an ache in my heart. I bear the scars of many wayward travels, painful journeys through grasping briars and dark forests. Places where I came to believe no one could really rescue me—or no one would want to. For, oh my goodness, if people really knew who I was, what I was like! If people could see my great lack, hear my silly mumblings—this broken girl huddled in a pile, bruised and broken. Was I even worth rescuing?

My Father thought so. He never gave up on me.

And when I finally stopped running, he was right there, ready to wrap his loving arms around me and carry me back home where I belong.

Just as you thought—a lost girl found.

But there's a twist to this particular story.

You see, it's not about an unbeliever who finds Jesus after years of wandering and is saved. Because when this story happened, I already knew Jesus. I was already saved. In fact, I was the quintessential good Christian girl.

I grew up in the church and learned Scripture along with my ABCs. I accepted Christ at a young age and attended a Christian college, even took my fair share of theology courses. And I still needed rescuing.

When I was growing up in a conservative Baptist church, I loved to hear the testimonies of those whose lives were broken and painful before they came to the Lord. As an adult I loved them even more—these heart-touching tales from those who were lost and then found, those whose lives were changed by an encounter with the ever-gracious Savior. They're wonderful, juicy true-makeover stories with irresistible happy endings. The trouble is, the "before" in those stories is almost always "before I knew Christ." And the implication is that once a person accepts the Lord, she stops sinning and lays all her brokenness outside the door. The implication is that churches are populated by those who are joyfully and triumphantly healed.

And that's just not true—or it's just a fraction of the reality most good Christian girls I know experience. Most Christians know that. We'll admit it if we're pressed. We'll even make a point of telling people that "we're all sinners." Yet we're pretty quick to cover up our deeper failings. There are things we'll confess and others we don't dare mention to anyone—even, sometimes, to ourselves.

Why the cover-up? We tell ourselves we must "keep a good witness"—you know, keep God looking good. More often, I think, we do it to keep ourselves comfortable. To help us feel safe. Because we don't know how to handle pain or because, deep down, we're not sure if God can really handle who we really are and what we've really done.

Remember how the little girl in the woods thought she had found her father? But the father was really the one who found her. He was the hero of the story. And that's true for me.

Because my true bottom-line confession is not that I've been lost, but that I keep being found.

Not that I strayed and messed up, but that I've been rescued and given another chance . . . and another . . . and another.

Not that I'm a good Christian girl, but that I serve a good God.

And that I'm growing in his grace—with a lot of help—to be the woman God always wanted me to be.

A word of grace to all good Christian girls: come home to Christ. And he'll do all the rest.

It Is Time

Angela Thomas (*When Wallflowers Dance*)

Maybe you have lost your way. Maybe you've only been surviving the past few years. Or maybe you have become the un-woman with the un-life. I imagine that you've already tried a million things to overcome your emptiness. A fresh attitude. Getting up early to pray. A Bible study that might have the answer. A low-carb diet. The newest yoga class. A different church or a different job or a different husband. Maybe you've come to the end of your dreams and you refuse to try anything else—you've completely given up. Maybe you find yourself where I have been, sitting in the dark, despondent and desperate, praying that you'll just disappear.

Walking around on the earth is dangerous. Giving out your love can be painful. So many things come to us that steal our living. Disease, disappointment, busyness, consequences, circumstances, and failure. I understand why some moms begin drinking in secret to anesthetize their lives. I understand mind-numbing television watching or chick-lit novels or ridiculous shopping. Checking out can make a lot of sense in light of the heartache most women carry. The mind is screaming, *Get me out of here!* And it seems you can't get away from the pain.

Sometimes, when we have become the un-woman with the un-life, not feeling seems the only way, and sitting alone in the dark seems to be all that we deserve. But the soul desperately knows it was made for more. One of my favorite authors, Henri Nouwen, wrote about the truth of our spiritual condition:

> It often seems that the more I try to disentangle myself from the darkness, the darker it becomes. I need light, but that light has to conquer my darkness, and that I cannot bring about myself. I

cannot forgive myself. I cannot make myself feel loved. By myself I cannot leave the land of my anger. I cannot bring myself home nor can I create communion on my own. I can desire it, hope for it, wait for it, yes, pray for it. But my true freedom I cannot fabricate for myself. That must be given to me. I am lost. I must be found and brought home by the shepherd who goes out to me.[2]

Maybe you can't think anymore, your body is exhausted, and your heart has given up. Maybe you are weary of wandering through the years and tired of squinting through blurry vision. Maybe your soul has crawled into bed and cried itself to sleep. Maybe you need someone to come into your life, bend down to pick you up, and boldly say, "The Shepherd has found you. He is bringing you home. There will be dancing when you get there. Listen to me now. I am going to tell you exactly what to do."

Several years ago I came to understand that I am held by the lavish, never-ending love of God. That kind of love means there are no women relegated to wallflower lives. Day-to-day is very difficult for most of us, but we do not have to become the un-woman with the un-life. We do not have to numb down and go away. God intended so much more. The woman who belongs to God gets to dance. Inside the strength of his embrace, you can become the woman you have always wanted to be . . . the one he dreamed of when he dreamed of you.

Maybe your soul is sleepy. Maybe your heart aches

underneath all the burdens you carry. Maybe you have given up on ever becoming the woman you used to dream of being. Stay with me.

This day I want you to hear the truth. Your Creator has amazing plans that still lie in front of you. No matter what has come to you, the disappointments you have known, the consequences you have received, or the wounds that have kept you down. Even if you have truly failed or wasted a lot of precious time. Hear me shout this life-giving truth: it is never too late to dance with God!

He'll take your threadbare dreams and weave a tapestry called your purpose. He'll plow a brand-new road to lead you out of the lost place you've ended up.

God looks across the room at the un-woman who is giving up and fading away, the woman he has never stopped loving, and he asks that wallflower to dance.

Jesus said, I came to give life—life in all its fullness (John 10:10 NCV), and no woman who makes her life in Christ has to live empty.

The Delicious Stirring of Hope

Paula Rinehart (*Better Than My Dreams*)

In recent years I have begun to notice unexpected moments when I feel a delicious stirring of hope. It's a wild and unusual feeling, as it often occurs in situations that, humanly speaking, look pretty bleak.

Let me explain a little more. As a counselor, I listen to women share their stories all day long. I hear about the real stuff of their lives, which is not unlike my own. And as I listen to stories of, say, a father's death or a mother's drinking problem or a spouse's neglect, I am discovering that no matter what the specific circumstances may be, truly, we are all telling the same story—of loves and hopes, of our failures and our fears.

Our stories are like patchwork quilts we stitch together during seasons of joy or duress into a kind of security blanket we carry through life.

As I listen to a woman talk about her quilt, or as I consider my own, two words often come to mind: *But God.*

If, in trying to face our lives head-on, all we had in our hands were a few psychological tools and a smattering of the best human self-help, just how lost would we stay? How condemned would we be to an endless repeating of the same-old, same-old, stuck forever in a morass of (mostly) our own making?

But God.

Perhaps this is why such a wild hope is stirred in me. For what I hear now, in other women's stories, are the first rumblings of something I've stumbled upon myself.

The struggle is a door, and inside God waits. If you are willing to walk through the portal, you find what you could not experience deeply any other way. The gospel comes to life there. The power to forgive yourself and everybody else . . . a crack at discovering the way God actually redeems what seems irredeemable . . . the hope of seeing him create a new ending out of a bad beginning—it's all waiting to be fleshed out.

There is really Someone there, in whose company lies the love you have longed for since you took your first breath. He is waiting.

Part I

The Things That Keep Us Stuck

*"Let us throw off everything that hinders
and the sin that so easily entangles . . ."*

(Heb. 12:1 NIV)

Hiding in Guilt and Shame

Exposed

Sheila Walsh (*God Has a Dream for Your Life*)

I wonder what it felt like to be the woman in John's Gospel who had been caught in the act of adultery. Her face burning with shame, she was hauled in front of a crowd of so-called respectable people and exposed as a sinner. She had no defense. She had been caught in the act, and now her life was over. They made her stand there as they discussed her fate with this man.

Why were they letting this Jewish teacher decide what should happen to her? Who was this man? Her shame circled her like fire, separating her from decent people until he spoke. He gave out rock-throwing privileges to the first man among them who had never sinned. She was confused. There was a difference between the kind of sin that she committed and the kind that respectable people committed. Everyone knew that, didn't they?

He waited. She waited, her heart pounding like a hammer on wood, like a stone on flesh. One by one, they all walked away. He looked her in the eyes and asked if there was no one left to condemn her. She admitted that there was no one left because they had all disappeared like bats in the daylight.

His next sentence changed her forever: "I also don't judge you guilty. You may go now, but don't sin anymore" (John 8:11 NCV).

Chained by Guilt
Angela Thomas (*When Wallflowers Dance*)

Not so long ago a woman asked to have breakfast with me. She was single and had allowed herself to act inappropriately with a man she had been dating. Brokenhearted over her mistake, we sat together and sorted things out. She was mad at herself, frustrated by her poor choosing, and aching over her shame before the man and before God. We talked through her obvious repentance and prayed together, and I am sure that she received God's complete forgiveness that morning.

About eight months later she came to me again. Still grieving the same sin of that one night. Still flogging herself.

"Has anything happened since we last talked?" I asked. "Have you made similar choices again? Has that night become a pattern for you in any way?"

"No," she spoke through her tears. "It was just that one time, but I still live with such shame and regret. I'm reminded all the time of my blatant disobedience to God."

"Do you remember the morning that we prayed and asked God for his forgiveness?" I asked.

She nodded her head that she remembered.

"Then tell me what we have if the forgiveness of God does not truly forgive?"

My friend said nothing.

"Look at me," I gently persuaded. "You have been forgiven. Your conscience is clear. The accuser wants you to live in shame and weakness because of your mistake. Eight months have gone by, and you could have been living grateful for the forgiveness God has given. It's time to lift your head up. God has made you clean."

You can't do anything or accomplish anything or begin to grow in strength or confidence when your life is shackled to a wall of guilt. Darkness settles over the heaviness in your heart and holds you hostage there in the confusion. Your conscience is an instrument of the Holy Spirit. It's right to feel guilty over sin or poor choices. That good guilt can prompt us to seek forgiveness and restoration.

But if we choose not to immediately respond to the leading of the Holy Spirit, then our consciences can become so encumbered that we find our lives essentially chained to guilt we've tried to ignore. That kind of prolonged guilt begins to defile our thinking and our emotions.

We live in such a dark society that I think we've come to accept our society's darkness as an unavoidable part of our own. It can begin to feel as if we are required to pull this ball and chain of guilt and private struggle around with us. Besides, it seems everybody else does. But it does not have to be so. We belong to God, and he has made a way for us to live in the light. We can live with a clear conscience because of the freedom Christ gives. We can pursue a clean life even if no one else around us wants to go there and even if others continue to remind us of our mistakes. We do not have to be shackled to guilt and the shame of poor choices for a lifetime. Because of Jesus, we can serve God with a clear conscience.

This has possibly been one of the most difficult next-level truths of God for me to personally receive and apply. All the time God has been yelling to me, "I want to set you free! I want to make you clean. I'm sending a Savior. I am moving heaven and earth to get to you." And for most of my life I have rejected this kind of freedom from guilt.

Then I will sprinkle clean water on you, and you will be clean. I will cleanse you from all your uncleanness and your idols. (Ezek. 36:25 NCV)

Guilt seemed righteous somehow. And maybe if I just kept flogging myself before God, he would be happier with me because

THE THINGS THAT KEEP US STUCK

of my shame. God was probably always mad at me about something anyway, and it was my job to uncover what God would be mad at me about next. Besides, how in the world could anyone ever have and maintain a clear conscience? Sounds haughty and arrogant, like something only an apostle could say.

Come to find out, most women feel much the same way and struggle with the application of this truth. Most of the Christian women I know are smart enough not to choose poorly in public. Their shackles are private, and they spend inordinate amounts of time and energy trying to hold back the darkness they play with. As you know, darkness is a powerful element. It begins to take over from the inside out, eventually pushing out most of the light. It is very easy to wake up one sunny day, completely overtaken by the dark.

I'm going to list for you some of the chains I've heard about recently from women who whisper to me through their tears. As you read through these observations, I want you to pay special attention to any prompting the Holy Spirit might give to you.

- Women are having illicit sex, both single and married, young and old, Christian and non. And/or they are spending way more time than we've previously believed fantasizing about having an affair or an inappropriate relationship. We always used to think that was just for men.
- Many Christian women are involved in lesbian relationships, both sexual and emotional. Maybe they have not consummated their relationship with the physical act of sex, but their

emotional dependence has become an unhealthy attachment—an attachment that should have been reserved for a
husband in a marriage relationship.

- There is a dangerous proliferation of pornography weaving
  its way into the hearts and minds of women. The images are
  everywhere and so they almost seem normal to us now. Mag-
  azines, films, chat rooms, and the easy access on the Internet
  to information that no one needs. We would be deceived to
  believe that pornography is only a man's battle.

- Grown-up women are quietly suffering from eating disorders of all types, trapped inside the cage of "have to be thin
  at any cost."

- A snare that I have heard a lot about recently involves the
  private determination to get revenge. In relationships, careers, and families, women have found themselves entangled
  in a web they have woven by setting traps for others and plot-
  ting their private vindication.

- Deeply entrenched anger and all the emotional and physical by-products of its presence privately destroy the hearts
  of many.

- Reckless spending, gambling, prescription drug use, and alcohol abuse are chains that aren't quite as secret anymore.
  It's become very common for us to accept these activities in
  others or in ourselves.

I may not have touched on your particular private battle, but the question for all of us remains the same: Is your conscience clear?

Chained by Our Secrets

Jill Hubbard (*The Secrets Women Keep*)

Secrets are a way we hide our true selves from the world. Shame and fear keep us from letting others know who we really are, what mistakes we've made, and the ways we feel we don't measure up. Christian women especially seem to feel the need to hide the ways they're not perfect. We make bad choices like everyone else; we sin and sometimes turn our backs on God, but the idea of letting others know about the ways we fail strikes fear into our hearts. It's supremely *uncomfortable* for us to have our weaknesses, failings, or disappointments on parade for others to see.

Many of us keep secrets out of guilt over sin or failing. Unfortunately, the more we live in our guilt all alone, the easier it is for the enemy to use our guilt to keep us feeling shameful, unworthy, *not good enough*. We feel more and more like we're living in the dark, lonely and worthless. As long as we stay in the dark with our secrets, we allow the enemy to keep us feeling that way. Bringing our secrets out of the dark and into the light can allow us to gain perspective on them, see that we're not alone, and understand that regardless of how "bad" the secret is, it doesn't have to define us. We are still loved and lovable.

Shame On You

Sheila Walsh (*God Has a Dream for Your Life / Let Go*)

Jesus knew who the woman at the well was and what she had done, and he didn't judge her. Not only that, he gave her the chance to dream again.

"Don't do that anymore."
"Choose a different life."
"Be a different woman."
"Dream a bigger dream."

He talked as someone who knew what he was talking about, and he was giving her dreams another chance.

That is the hope for every one of us. The cross of Calvary is a place to drop our overcoats of shame. It is the place where all that is true about us and all that is false meet the grace and mercy of God.

Will you take a moment and consider your life?

Are there roots of shame interwoven with who you really are?

Have your dreams been crushed by a sense that you don't belong or you will never measure up?

Is it possible for you to believe that God knows everything
about you and loves and accepts you too?

Shame is like the cheap, cloying perfume that I used to get as a child at Christmastime. Mine came in a little bottle in the shape of a dog, which I loved, but the fragrance inside was terrible. One Christmas, as I opened the container and sniffed, hoping this year the manufacturer had come up with something more pleasant-smelling, my little brother ran past me with his new robot. He rammed into me at full throttle and the whole bottle poured out onto my sweater. The smell was atrocious! I took my sweater off, took a bath, and then I took another bath. But I smelled of that cheap perfume until Easter!

Shame is nauseating. It is heavy. Lewis Smedes, in his wonderful book *Shame and Grace*, described it as "a dead weight of not-good-enough-ness."[1] It is like a ravenous, demanding monster, and no matter how much you feed it to quiet the noise, it is never enough. It sits in the pit of your stomach or wraps its cold arms around your shoulders. And it doesn't let go.

Guilt tells me I have done something wrong. With that awareness there is hope. I can go to the person I have hurt and ask him or her to forgive me. Or I can work to right an injustice I committed. Shame, on the other hand, tells me I *am* something wrong. There is no hope there. Where do I go to change who I am at my core? How can I fix it?

Shame is a devastating sickness of the soul. It tells us not to show up. It tells us we don't belong. It tells us that if people knew who we really are, we would be asked to leave. Shame doesn't even have to make sense because it weighs so much and takes up so much space in our lives we don't even think to stop and question its right to be there. Guilt would have been the appropriate response of

Adam and Eve to their tragic disobedience in the garden of Eden, but shame was the hellish breath the serpent covered them with. Guilt can present a door, whereas shame is a dead end. But worst of all, shame offers no hope.

Letting Go and Receiving God's Grace

Tammy Maltby (*Confessions of a Good Christian Girl*)

Through my own lengthy process of learning what costly forgiveness is all about, even walking it through with others, and then ending the journey in my own backyard, I believe God has been showing me something of his heart. He's teaching me that honest pain can be healed, but secret, hidden pain cannot. And that when we truly take that truth to heart, we start living in a completely different way—a way that gives life to ourselves and those around us.

When we finally get honest with ourselves and others about just how lost we are, that's when we start to be found. It begins with the most loving and difficult of all acts: forgiving ourselves, embracing our humanness, and believing that somehow God can turn our brokenness into beauty. It begins with understanding the reality that Christ died for sinners, which means all of us—good Christian girls as well as those who don't know him at all. It begins when we open our eyes and our hearts in wonder to his grace.

Because, in the end, it's all about grace. Loving, forgiving grace. Passionate, overwhelming, truly amazing grace.

Breaking the Shackles

Angela Thomas (*When Wallflowers Dance*)

If you want a clear conscience, God makes it simple. Ask, receive, and then choose to live clean, being made clean again and again by the ongoing process of repentance and receiving God's forgiveness.

Here's the hard part. For many of us, a clear conscience is going to take some work. There is a lot of cleaning that needs to happen. There is a whole lot more going on than just not receiving God's forgiveness eight months ago or eight years ago. My friend Mark Pate says there are two types of sin: 1) not obeying, which is the sin of rebellion; and 2) the sin of presumption, or going ahead when God has not issued a directive, which always has consequences.

Whether it's the sin of disobedience or presumption, there are sin patterns to deal with, core beliefs that have to be radically changed, and a lifestyle that must be transformed with the truth of God's call to clean living. Not so many are up for the work. Either we are going to grow up and become mature women, or we are going to remain whiny, saved but sloppy, spiritually going around in circles, watching the days of our empty lives go by.

There are things God has asked us not to do because we belong to him. We carry inside these vessels the living presence of the Holy Spirit. We have been set apart and called to be different. We reflect his heart to a very lost and sick world. At the very least we cannot come to believe it's okay to continue in our sin. We cannot act like the rest of the world.

We have not been called to blend in, looking and sounding just like we did before we knew Christ. Don't you remember? We live in this world, but we are no longer of this world. People should be able to tell the difference. It takes a lot of mental calisthenics and emotional energy to cover an unclean conscience or blatant choices that go against the heart of God.

When you and I allow darkness or choose darkness, we are also choosing to remain spiritually immature. It's virtually impossible to go forward with God when you are spending most of your time covering what keeps you unclean.

Maybe God has already begun the work of discipline in your life. Maybe you are suffering the consequences of poor choices. If your conscience is not clear, if you find yourself trapped inside a private world that is out of control or out of order, or if you aren't sure that you have ever stood clean before God, here's what I want you to do.

Begin by reading the following verses from the Bible. Listen to God affirm his desire that we live with a clear conscience.

So, I strive always to keep my conscience clear before God and man. (Acts 24:16 NIV)

Now this is our boast: Our conscience testifies that we have conducted ourselves in the world, and especially in our relations with you, in the holiness and sincerity that are from God. We have done so not according to worldly wisdom but according to God's grace. (2 Cor. 1:12 NIV)

How much more is done by the blood of Christ. He offered himself through the eternal Spirit as a perfect sacrifice to God. His blood will make our consciences pure from useless acts so we may serve the living God. (Heb. 9:14 NCV)

Next is the choice to surrender to the process of being made clean. I realize this is probably uncomfortable for you. But sometimes it's necessary for a season.

1. Begin with self-examination. Where are you with God today? What stands in between you and a clear conscience? If you begin to peel back the layers of patterns and habits you've developed over the years, will you find sin that has been hidden or covered?

2. Confess your sin. Private confession for private sins. Public confession for public sins. All sin confessed to God. Private confession happens one-on-one with the one you have offended or hurt. That private confession may need to happen in front of a counselor or in front of a board of elders. But either way, the private confession of private sin remains private. Public confession is required when your disobedience has publicly caused harm to others and to your reputation. The newspaper journalist who has lied in her published reporting would not just confess to her editor. A public confession is required.

There was a time for me when I felt split open from head to toe. I remember begging God to show me anything else. While we were in there looking underneath my pretending, I asked him to go even deeper and show me anything and everything that kept me from him. When I am in my private time of confession with God, there is no reason to hold back. I want to be clean, and this process is the only way to get there.

John Ortberg has said, "Confession is not just naming what we have done in the past. It involves our intentions about the future as well. It requires a kind of promise."[2]

3. Ask for forgiveness. To confess is one step, but the humbling that comes in asking God's forgiveness is an act of obedience that cleanses. To ask for what we do not deserve also becomes a mile marker of sorts. One that reminds us where we don't want to go again.

4. Receive the mercy. God delights to show mercy. He delights to hold back what you and I have deserved. Receive this gift with gratefulness. God's mercy redeems your life. Listen to the truth of these words and their promise for your life:

Redemption is God bringing good out of bad, leading us to wholeness, and the experience of God's amazing power. Redemption means that out of our greatest pain, can come our most profound personal mission in life. [3]

God can take your confession and do the amazing work of redemption. He can make your life clean and then give purpose to your personal mission. But in order for all that to happen, things really do have to change.

You and I can't stay in the old patterns of deceit and expect to live pure. We can't hang out with the people who led us down the path. We can't visit the same old places anymore. We have to choose light over darkness and have nothing to do with the one who can lure us back with the same old tricks. If it feels like darkness, then it probably is. Choose the light. We remain unclean because we don't want to stay surrendered to examination, confession, and forgiveness. I understand. It's one of the hardest and best things I do.

I realize this piece of spiritual maturity can be painful and embarrassing. But to continue in an unclean life will bring us to an immediate dead end. There won't be any more growth apart from choosing to live clean. No confidence. No dancing. No grown-up woman with a great, big life. You will never even hear the music.

This day, run into the arms of God. Pray for his tender guidance. Ask him for a clear conscience and let him make you clean.

Here's how I have come to feel about the pursuit of a clear conscience. Either the forgiveness that God has promised to us is halfhearted and conditional, based on some unattainable, unknown standard of self-flogging and sustained guilt, or his forgiveness really forgives—instantly, eternally, and completely.

Either I believe that forgiveness is what God said—free, available to any who would call on his name, and completely able to cleanse the impure heart—or I don't really believe God. Either God can make you clean or he is not God.

I am staking my whole life on the belief that God is who he says he is. Jesus is really God's Son, my Savior. His death was enough to pay the penalty for every sin. His resurrection was the proof of his divinity. The Holy Spirit is the promised gift to you and me for day-by-day, moment-to-moment guidance. And for some reason that doesn't make any sense to anybody, God is so crazy in love with his creation that he freely forgives any who would ask. In case you haven't thought about it lately, when the God of heaven and earth forgives there is nothing that can happen to make it less, and there is nothing you can do to make it more. Forgiven in the name of Jesus means your conscience is clear.

That truth is why we get down on our hands and knees and worship the only One who is able to cleanse us from all unrighteousness. That's why we show up at church and persuade our friends to come to Bible studies and try to rearrange our lives around God. That's what makes God amazing and takes our breath away at God's generosity. That is why we sing and lift our hands to thank God for the gift of being forgiven. When God bends down in his mercy and forgives a helpless, little, beat-up woman like you or me, then no matter what anyone says or how many voices you hear in your head or how long it takes you to believe it, you have been made clean. You are forgiven.

It's time to hold your head up.

Holding on to
Our Broken Dreams

The Pictures in Our Heads

Paula Rinehart (*Better Than My Dreams*)

By my mid-thirties, I had become one of the most disillusioned Christians I've known, then or since. I worked hard to keep my skepticism quiet, as it felt distinctly like a virus that others might catch. If someone had asked me what was wrong, though, I could have offered only a vague response. "I'm not sure . . . Life just isn't working out like I planned."

But did you have a plan exactly?

"Well, no," I would have replied. "But God had a plan, didn't he? You know what they say: 'God loves you and has a wonderful plan for your life.'" And then I might have added under my breath that my present experience didn't qualify as anybody's standard definition of *wonderful.*

So no, I didn't exactly have a plan . . . but I did have distinct pictures in my mind of how I thought my life would look. Through the hazy outlines of the future I saw everything with a golden glow— marriage to a man who could complete my unspoken thoughts and children who lined up their lives as neatly as their shoes. I wanted a vibrant ministry to women and a quiet, lovely house on a hill. And I thought God would offer some sort of immunity from anything that deeply disturbed this happy picture.

As you step out into life, the heat gets turned up on your dreams and desires and expectations. Your longings surface—as, indeed, they are meant to. Perhaps you didn't know you wanted a baby so much, for example, until you could not get pregnant. You might have felt the longing to be married more intensely as good men seemed in short supply. Life has a way of awakening our hearts in big ways, and pain of some sort is usually the megaphone.

Who among us travels very far in life without running headlong into the gap between what we hoped for and what came to pass?

The Plans We Make

Angela Thomas (*A Beautiful Offering*)

When I was a little girl in North Carolina dreaming about what I wanted to be when I grew up, I chose the most radical, adventurous, outside-my-box, scare-my-parents-silly thing I could think of. My mom was a nurse and my dad sold produce. I was their firstborn, and I decided that I wanted to be an astronaut. Of course, no one took me seriously for a while, which made me all the more determined.

I kept talking about being an astronaut and reading books on NASA and lunar landings. In the third grade, I sat riveted to watch all the *Apollo* coverage on our grainy black-and-white television. While the other girls were doing book reports on cats or manners, I always chose topics such as space and moon rocks and exploration. I would stir up a glass of Tang for breakfast and think about what it would be like to drink it through a straw while floating upside down in a space suit. We built model rockets at school once, and I was thrilled to get out of that stupid sewing module and onto my life's calling. I knew I'd eventually prove to all the naysayers that I was serious. I didn't know you needed to be a genius to be an astronaut; I thought you just had to want to. And if it was about "want to," then I had it.

One Christmas I asked for and received a telescope so that I could keep an eye on things and chart my course through the stars. Never mind that it was the dinkiest little tabletop telescope ever, with three wobbly legs. I took it outside at dusk and stared at the moon.

Soon I had convinced all the neighborhood kids that I could see the United States flag Neil Armstrong and Buzz Aldrin had planted on the lunar surface during the *Apollo 11* mission. I was so sure that I even convinced myself I could see it. I can still remember blurry images of red, white, and blue and my big-shot attitude. "If you were astronaut material, you'd be able to see the flag," I'd argue.

I think that right this very moment is the first time I am consciously realizing that I probably did not actually see the Stars and Stripes from my front yard. This is a hard revelation. But how could you see a flag on the moon with a couple of scratched-up lenses inside a white plastic tube? I guess you can't. How embarrassing. I haven't thought about this in forever, and it's kind of painful to realize I've believed my own hype all these years. A grand imagination dies a bitter, slow death, you know.

I bet you've already guessed where this story is going. One day some know-it-all said, "You can't be an astronaut. Astronauts need perfect vision. You can't wear glasses when you blast off in a rocket. They don't stay on in zero gravity." I'd never heard of such a thing. Then I checked around, and sure enough, back then, it was true. There were no four-eyed astronauts.

How could my best idea for an awe-inspiring, adventurous life be instantly gone? What was I going to do? The big dream inside this skinny girl was shattered. That dream had made me important. Everybody thought I had courage. How was I going to be somebody with no wild, over-the-top career to aspire to?

It was a very difficult day when my astronaut dream broke.

Fast-forward about ten years, and that same nerdy girl meets Jesus in college. Thankfully there were no vision requirements except spiritual eyes to see. Maybe for the first time since the astronaut dream died, I had a reason to live. But I was still me, and I brought my energetic, wait-till-you-see-what-I-can-do-for-Jesus attitude to our relationship.

I thought it would work out great. Jesus needed me to show everybody how to be a model, happy Christian, and I needed something to do with my life since I wouldn't be going to the moon. I really fell in love with God and jumped into my new reason to live with both of my busy feet. I was a quick learner. Just give me the instructions, tell me what the rules are, then stand back and watch. I was going to be the best little Christian girl Jesus ever had.

And you know that whole thing kind of worked for a while. I am predisposed toward happy. I like happy people, and I like to make people happy. So my being happy for Jesus was a good fit. It gave me energy. It propelled me through seminary and the first years of my ministry. It was almost as if nothing could hurt me in those days. I had wanted the world to know about Jesus and the happy life they could have in him. What I didn't realize was that life out there in the real world was eventually going to roll in and teach me a thing or two about happy. Make that roll right over on top of me. No, more like put me under an asphalt paver and squish me flat like a bug, you know, where the guts are everywhere and you can't even tell what it used to be? Yep, that's about how it was somewhere around my early thirties.

Maybe as the happy Jesus girl, I had all the right motives and exactly the right approach for those years, but I was blissfully ignorant about the pain and disappointment that can come to each of us. Before I really knew what was happening, parts of my life began to crack and little pieces started to break off and smash flat.

It was an even more difficult day when my perfect-Jesus-girl dream broke.

Wanting Life on Our Terms

Paula Rinehart (*Better Than My Dreams*)

Dreams and expectations in life, especially in our culture, have a curious way of inflating. Simple hope can harden into expectation and even demand. We live in an atmosphere of demand, where a problem is something to be solved, not endured, and suffering is seen as an intruder. We are told over and over that our lives should be a certain way—and we each have our own notions of what that looks like.

The irony is that this drift from hope . . . to expectation . . . to demand is a trap that is much easier to fall into as a Christian. C.S. Lewis was right: coming into a relationship with Jesus is, indeed, like falling out of the back of a wardrobe into the fresh wonder of a whole new world where anything can happen. Aren't we all acquainted with Jesus' words "with God all things are possible" (Matt. 19:26 NASB)? It's so easy to fill in the blank called "all things" with a script God never quite had in mind—or to assume that knowing Jesus will somehow spare you a heartache he actually intends to walk you through.

When our sticky fingers get wrapped around our dreams—when hope has mutated into an agenda that God is supposed to fulfill—then we are living from a place of entitlement. What I'm saying is that the virus of entitlement will eventually steal from you nearly everything that's good. It will bar the door to a genuine, honest experience with God that includes the best of times—and some of the worst—all in the same container.

Inflated expectations take you to an artificial place. They can work a real number on the way you see God. For when your life does not play out like the movie in your mind—when there's divorce or infertility, rejection, or betrayal in your path—God may look more like Scrooge, withholding something you vitally need. He's let you down. He's left you by the side of the road to fend for yourself. That's the darker side of where we go when we cling to this invisible demand of entitlement.

When I suspect the presence of this virus in my life, I am often drawn to a piercingly accurate comment made by a man of the faith many years ago. I've never forgotten his words. J. B. Phillips, one of the first translators of the New Testament into modern English, wrote this:

> The people who feel that God is a disappointment have not understood the terms on which we inhabit this planet.[1]

lips is saying that for true joy and hope to take hold of us, we have to begin from an altogether different place. We must understand the terms on which we inhabit this planet. This is a broken world, riddled with heartache, in desperate search of a Savior—not "a well-run kindergarten where good is rewarded and evil punished."[2]

I am not living in the land of neat packages.

The actual starting place—the terms on which we inhabit the planet—is closer to the prophet Jeremiah's take on things. "It is of the Lord's mercies that we are not consumed," he said (Lam. 3:22 KJV). No sense of entitlement there! Nothing is a given, really, not even my next breath. We are not in a position to demand. It's all a gift. That's a very different orientation to life and to God, but it is true north. Follow that path and gratitude will not be far behind.

It Depends on Where You Are Standing

Sheila Walsh (*God Has a Dream for Your Life*)

When I lived in London, I decided to take a trip to Land's End. The scenery is spectacular with magnificent cliffs overlooking the Atlantic Ocean. It's quite breathtaking. You need a good head for heights to be able to go anywhere near the edge of these fabled cliffs.

As I stood there that day, looking out across the ocean to the French coast, I had a little epiphany. I discovered that my position altered my perspective significantly. If I stood with my back to England, looking down over the jagged edges to the water below, I had come to the end. There was nowhere else to go. But if I turned around and had my back to the ocean, I looked out across the lush fields of Cornwall and had the whole country in front of me. I was just beginning, and I could go almost anywhere.

I think it is the same with our dreams. When a dream dies, we can fix our gaze solely on what lies behind in the dust, or with God's help, we can turn around and dream a new dream.

I believe that dreams should be honored even if they were foolish or unfulfilled. When I look back at some of the things I dreamed for as a child, it is easy to ridicule or dismiss them. I think we do too much of that as women. We are so critical of ourselves. My prayer for you today at this place in your journey is for a fresh experience of the grace of God. You would not be the woman you are today, with all that is beautiful and kind and strong in you, if you had not come along the very path that you did.

Broken dreams should be given time to be mourned. We live in such a fast-paced culture that we often don't give our hearts time to catch up with our bodies. I wonder how many sicknesses are actually our bodies telling us that we are not doing well. When we take time to mourn what has come to an end, then we are ready for God to meet us with the next step in our journey.

osing to Believe

ıgela Thomas (*When Wallflowers Dance*)

I met a new friend a few years ago. He is a lanky mid-fiftyish guy with a very intense, very secular eighty-hour-a-week career. He is divorced from a mean woman and for ten years he has lived alone, trying to co-parent with someone no one would want to deal with. His children are mad at their mother, and because of it, they've given him plenty of heartache. But the day I met this man, he came through the door happy. I'm not kidding, he was genuinely happy.

This very unassuming, ordinary-to-look-at man stands apart in character and countenance. So happy, in fact, that just his presence lights up every room we've ever been in. Not only that, we're now three years into meetings and programs, and in every encounter we've ever had, his spirit has been consistently and remarkably the same. Peaceful and positive and looking for good. He's fun to be with. All his colleagues hold him in high esteem. He is respected in his profession and regarded as wise and insightful. The man is not bitter, and he's just like you or me—he's got a hundred reasons he could give in to.

One day I took him to lunch to ask the burning questions, "Where in the world did your countenance come from? Are you always happy?"

"Angela, do you think I have a happy-go-lucky, carefree life without any sadness?"

"No, I realize that your life circumstances have been difficult. That's why I'm so interested in hearing about your heart and your thinking. I have rarely met someone like you. Your spirit is full. You radiate a light that touches everyone you meet. Tell me what it is."

"I believe God."

"Somehow, I knew you were going to say that."

Every time I have ever allowed myself to fall into bitterness and disappointment, I realize that I have listened to the prompting of Satan. I have inclined my head toward his directives. I have forgotten that my God is on the throne of all creation. His heart toward me is good. His promises are true. His Son is my Savior. I have forgotten to live what I believe.

Maybe that's where you are today. You realize that you aren't believing God. Maybe you have every earthly right to feel bitter and resentful, but it's been long enough now. It's time to let go of this sickly method of coping. You desire the way out. You want to dance with God toward his plans and his purpose. You want to know a genuine happiness that circumstances cannot stain.

God's New Dream for Your Life

Sheila Walsh (*God Has a Dream for Your Life*)

Are you ready to discover God's dream for your life and take off flying like the wind? Think back on who you were as a little girl.

What were the things that you loved to do more than anything else? What were the moments that made you feel alive, as if this were what you were placed on this earth to do? I joke with my young son that throughout my elementary school years, I was punished for talking in class. Now it is my life.

What were the things about you that stood out? Did you line up your dolls and teach them or make things with your hands? Could you run faster than anyone in your class? I love the line from the movie *Chariots of Fire* when the lead character, Eric Liddell, says, "I believe God made me for a purpose, but he also made me fast. And when I run, I feel his pleasure."[3]

That is a profoundly spiritual statement. We think that ministry or worship is something that only happens on Sunday mornings or Wednesday nights. But God asks us to bring everything we have to the table and offer it as an act of worship every day. Each one of us is given only one life—your days on earth are not a dress rehearsal so that you can come back and try again. Every life counts. Your life counts.

You may be reading this and thinking, *That's easy for you to say as you travel all over the country to speak to thousands of women while dressed in fine suits and tripping over your four-inch heels. But I've got three kids, a bad back, and a husband who snores!* Well, first of all, bless your heart! I will say a little prayer for you. Second, that's irrelevant. Your life as it is today matters to God. Why else would he have assigned angels to watch over you at all times? "For He shall give His angels charge over you, to keep you in all your ways. In their hands they shall bear you up, lest you dash your foot against a stone" (Ps. 91:11–12 NKJV).

Heaven is watching us to see what we will do with the life we have been given.

Perhaps as you think about this, you are convinced that you have blown your chance. You know without a shadow of a doubt that God called you to do something with your life, but you messed up, so it's too late. Think again.

We get funny ideas of what it looks like to be a godly woman. We think that God's dream for our lives would have us running around like spiritual versions of Wonder Woman:

- "Today, I will learn three chapters of the New Testament while knitting blankets for the poor. Then after breakfast, I will lead two neighbors to Christ. One will become a missionary in China, while the other will get hit by a Mack truck before reaching the supermarket, therefore bypassing the produce aisle and going straight to heaven!
- "After lunch, I will visit my mother-in-law in the nursing home. I will laugh at her good-humored-yet-hurtful comments about the color of my hair and then lead all the residents in a time of worship. After supper, my son and I will build a life-size working model of Mount Vesuvius erupting for his science project.
- "Tonight, I will give my husband his slippers, which I purchased with the money saved by returning soda bottles, and

then I'll take the trash out, understanding that he's had a long day and the last thing he needs is to hear me nagging. Finally, I will leap into bed, thanking God for another day as Wonder Woman!"

If we have tried that and failed, we think our only alternative is to quit! But when we take another trip back to the Garden of Eden, it is clear that God's dream for our lives has nothing to do with our performance. It has everything to do with our hearts. Fortunately, God doesn't quit believing in us even after we've stopped believing in ourselves. If God gave up on people who have failed, then Eve, Moses, Esther, David, Simon Peter, Mary Magdalene, and countless others would never have been used by him. In fact, God couldn't use anybody if he didn't use broken vessels.

Adam was formed from the dust outside the garden, but Eve was created from his side. As Martin Luther observed, God could have made Eve from Adam's toe to be lorded over or from his head to rule him, but he made her from his side to be his equal and companion. As a result of their sin, Adam and Eve were banished from that place of perfection and had to leave many of their dreams in the dust.

We, too, live in a fallen world where all our dreams do not come true. We know that. But I want to remind you . . . it's not over yet. When we have come to the end of ourselves, God is waiting to give us a new dream.

3

Living in Disobedience

Mad About the Narrow Road

Angela Thomas (*A Beautiful Offering*)

I have a friend who ponders God with great devotion. She reads feverishly and always wants to discuss her new insights into God's character. All of her growing-up life, she has been consumed with the idea that we have to live a life that is pleasing to God—out of duty. And all of her life she has felt that she comes up short. She wants to offer a beautiful life back to God, but she thinks that nothing she can give is good enough.

She thinks that God is mad at her. She believes that when she sins, he turns his back on her. She feels as if he must be a cosmic state trooper who writes wide-path citations, continues to tabulate bad points for her record, and can't wait to catch her sinning enough that he can finally take away her license to enjoy life.

We have talked and talked and talked about the net of grace. She says, "I hear you," but she can't find any rest. She has this notion that God requires a perfect offering. I say, "Well, he did require a perfect offering. That was Jesus. Now, because of Jesus, we can come to God, in our imperfection, and be received as beautiful."

My friend has swung from both sides of the pendulum. For years, she kept the rules and that didn't work, and then sometime after college, she broke all the rules and felt awful. The narrow path makes her mad and the wide path destroys her life. People don't like thinking that the life God blesses is through a narrow gate, down a narrow path. Most of us want the interstate life with lots of room to weave in and out, a variety of exits and options, and never any citations for driving recklessly. Most of us just want to live any way we please. We'd like to apply all the grace verses and disregard all the narrow-road verses. Thankfully, with God, both come wrapped in the same package. The call toward the narrow gate is given inside the gracious embrace of God's love and protection:

Enter through the narrow gate. For wide is the gate and broad is the road that leads to destruction, and many enter through it. But small is the gate and narrow the road that leads to life, and only a few find it. (Matt. 7:13–14 NIV)

I think that a lot of the people I know would like to enter through the narrow gate and then take the wide road. They believe that Jesus is the only way to be saved and they want that, but they'd prefer to avoid all his living instructions and make the rest of their journey on a superhighway. There are believers who know better and still choose to take the wide road. They live however they please with a few church services thrown in for good measure.

All my Christian friends who are taking the wide path are miserable. I mean it. They can't figure out what in the world is wrong. They have been called to the narrow path but want the wide path and its seeming enticements. They spend hours in therapy trying to reconcile the crazy roads they're taking. They are frustrated with God for not coming through . . . again, on the wide road. And they're wasting a whole lot of years in flat-out disobedience, wrecking their hearts and their calling.

There is such a conflict going on in their souls. The Holy Spirit has taken up residence, and his job is to give step-by-step direction for living. We take the narrow path every time we choose to respond to the Holy Spirit in obedience. The wide path keeps us in opposition to his leading. It's painful to watch my friends struggle with this truth. They believe that they deserve to be free, and it's out there somewhere beyond the guardrails of God's protection.

Jesus said that you can't live however you please and enjoy his kingdom blessings. I think that makes some people mad. And they'll probably be even madder when I tell them that the wide road is a mark of spiritual immaturity. Kicking and screaming to live however you please is the sign of a baby Christian. A small faith. Lack of understanding.

Sometimes it just doesn't make sense to us, so we try to figure out another way. We want to be free, so we run away from God. We choose all the things that keep us on the wide path and then one day we wake up and realize that we are in bondage, prisoners to our disobedience. But when we choose the narrow gate and the narrow road and hide ourselves in the shelter of his strong embrace, then we are finally free. I know it's hard to get your head around. But it's true. We desire the freedom that Jesus says comes from obedience. But we don't believe that the freedom could really be born of obedience, so we run toward bondage and hope there is an alternate route.

Now that will make you crazy.

Choosing the Path

Stormie Omartian (*Finding Peace for Your Heart*)

"When will I ever get to the point when I don't hurt inside?" I asked God one day in prayer. Even though I had been set free from depression and my life was far more stable than it had ever been, I still lived on an emotional roller coaster. My questions to God during that time went on and on:

"When will I stop feeling like a failure?"

"When will I not be devastated by what other people say to me?"

"When will I not view every hint of misfortune as the end of the world?"

"When will I be able to go through the normal occurrences of life without being traumatized by them?

There were no answers from God at that moment, but as I read the Bible the next morning, my eyes fell on the words, "Why do you call me 'Lord, Lord,' and not do the things which I say?" (Luke 6:46 NKJV). The passage went on to explain that anyone who hears the word of the Lord and does *not* put it into practice is building a house with no foundation. When the storm comes, it will collapse and be completely destroyed.

Could it be that I'm getting blown over and destroyed by every wind of circumstance that comes my way because I'm not doing what the Lord says to do in some area? I wondered. I knew I was building on solid rock (Jesus), and I had been laying a strong foundation (in the Word, prayer, praise, confession, and ongoing forgiveness), but it appeared that this foundation could only be stabilized and protected through my obedience.

I searched the Bible for more information, and every place I turned I read more about the rewards of obeying God:

Blessed are those who hear the word of God and keep it! (Luke 11:28 NKJV)

No good thing will He withhold from those who walk uprightly.
(Ps. 84:11 NKJV)

Behold, I set before you today a blessing and a curse: the blessing,
if you obey the commandments of the LORD your God which I
command you today. (Deut. 11:26–27 NKJV)

The more I read, the more I saw the link between *obedience* and the
presence of God.

"If anyone loves Me, he will keep My word; and My Father will
love him, and We will come to him and make Our home with
him" (John 14:23 NKJV).

The Trouble with Temptation
Sheila Walsh (*Let Go*)

The desert can be a cruel place. Barren and hot during the day, bit-
terly cold at night, empty of sustenance. It's not a place you or I
would choose to spend much time—at least not without basic crea-
ture comforts. Yet we find more than once that God used the desert
for his purposes.

Take the children of Israel. As told in Exodus, following some
devastating choices, they ended up wandering around the desert for
forty years. They had just been released from bondage in Egypt and

had been given the promise of a new life. Their story reads like a Shakespearian tragedy. I find myself holding my breath at each turn of the page. *Will they get it right this time? Will they finally choose the right path, or will they take another wrong turn that will lead them deeper and deeper into despair? Can't they see what they are doing? Will they never learn?*

In their desire for immediate gratification, the Israelites repeatedly turned from God. Time after time they gave in to temptation and suffered the consequences—for forty years!

Every day we struggle to say no to things that trip us up or yes to things we know are right. Why is that? Because like the Israelites, we're selfish. Simply put, we want what we want, and we'd really like it now. It's human nature, and it harkens back to that tasty morsel of fruit in the Garden of Eden. Over time and by God's grace we learn to temper our selfish nature, but some vestige of it still lurks under the surface.

Of course, different things tempt each of us. For some of us (okay, a lot of us) it's food. We crave food when we are happy, when we are sad, and when we can't quite make up our minds what we are. We gorge ourselves again and again until we can't move.

For others, it is relationships. We search for the perfect man who will fill the empty space inside us. We demand a certain ideal and won't settle for anything less, even if it means we might spend a lot of time alone.

For some, it is the temptation to dwell on the past and not move on to all that God has for us. Perhaps we feel if we move on we'll be letting go of something that is part of who we are. For many of us, the past is a golden age we grasp for, forgetting all the future might hold for us.

Whatever the temptation, the common thread will be the amount of time and energy involved in dealing with it—which is what Satan wants. A person preoccupied with herself is a person not preoccupied with God.

Understanding Obedience
Sheila Walsh (*Let Go*)

As we see in his letter to the church in Rome, Paul expressed the common cry of every believer who tries to live up to the standards of the law and fails miserably: "What I will to do, that I do not practice; but what I hate, that I do . . . O wretched man that I am! Who will deliver me from this body of death?" (Rom. 7:15, 24 NKJV). It is so easy to take the word of the law and miss the heart.

I believe there is a gulf between the law given by God to protect his people and the legalism that has such a death grip on the lives of many believers today. The law comes from the heart of a loving God who wants to protect his people—and is translated on our part into both loving obedience and a desire to encourage and help others. Legalism comes from a cold insistence by those who want to enforce their standards on everyone else.

The first five books of the Old Testament—Genesis, Exodus,

Leviticus, Numbers, and Deuteronomy—are known collectively as the Pentateuch, or the books of the Law. As we examine the laws given by God to his people, they reveal much more than rules; they reveal God's heart. God prefaced the Ten Commandments by restating his relationship with his children: "I am the LORD your God, who rescued you from slavery in Egypt" (Ex. 20:2 NLT).

When you look at these ten laws again (or for the first time), it seems like they shouldn't have been that difficult to follow. Think about it: Honor God and keep him first. Take a day off. Honor your mom and dad. Don't kill anyone. Don't sleep with anyone else's husband. Don't shoplift. Tell the truth. And if your friend has a nice new Coach purse, be happy for her!

God wasn't demanding twenty hours of community service every day or six hours of hymn singing before bedtime. He just wanted a few things that on first examination should have come naturally. The tragedy is that the Ten Commandments brought into sharp focus our complete inability to obey God in our own strength. The people of Israel just couldn't do it. They couldn't obey the law because . . . *they were sinners*. Just like us.

In this day of self-help gurus and feel-good books, it's easy to get away from the truth that we are all sinners. We were born into sin as children of Adam and Eve . . . and our culture does not want to hear about it. Look on the best-seller list and you'll find book after book that encourages us to believe we are the light of the world, we are like gods, and all we have to do is embrace that. That is a demonic lie. Our freedom doesn't come from becoming God but by embracing what God has done for us through his Son, Jesus Christ.

Jesus told us that if we follow him, we won't stumble around in the dark because he will give us his light to lead us (John 8:12–14). There is a huge gap between *following* the Light of the world and *being* the light of the world. It's not popular to talk about sin, but it's the truth.

When you break down the Ten Commandments, all God was asking us to do was to love him and to love one another. Does that sound familiar? Remember when the scribes and Pharisees in Jesus' day accused him of destroying the law?

When the Pharisees heard how he had bested the Sadducees, they gathered their forces for an assault. One of their religion scholars spoke for them, posing a question they hoped would show him up: "Teacher, which command in God's Law is the most important?" Take a look at what Jesus said when they tried to trip him up:

> "Love the Lord your God with all your passion and prayer and intelligence." This is the most important, the first on any list. But there is a second to set alongside it: "Love others as well as you love yourself." These two commands are pegs; everything in God's Law and the Prophets hangs from them. (Matt. 22:37–40 MSG)

Jesus' response clarifies the difference between legalism and the law. The Pharisees were legalists, trying to impress God by following the letter of the law. But Jesus' surprising answer was this: God was looking at their hearts, not their rule books.

Giving Our All

Marilyn Meberg (*God at Your Wits' End*)

Scripture, our faith object, teaches that it is God who is in control of everything on earth and in heaven: "I know, LORD, that a person's life is not his own. No one is able to plan his own course" (Jer. 10:23 NLT).

It is impossible to wiggle past this gigantic truth: God is in control of all things. He is sovereign. On a human level, one who is sovereign is a king or a queen, a ruler. He or she has all the power. On a divine level, God is our Ruler: God has all the power. No one reigns over him.

Our task is to give up our desire for control and relinquish our will into the sovereign hands of God. Scripture certainly makes God's divine kingship clear, but many of us continue to fuss about the word *all*, even as we attempt to acknowledge that God is sovereign and hand him our wills. When God says he is in control of "all" things, we get a little argumentative and say, "Surely God does not mean absolutely everything. Surely there are a few things we're in control of."

Were those my thoughts, I'd be guilty of faulty thinking. God is not just a *trifle* sovereign; he does not just have a *touch* of sovereignty. He is totally sovereign. That means we have to drag back the word *all* and think it . . . believe it . . . trust it . . . and have faith in the One who enables our faith.

Free to Obey
Angela Thomas (*A Beautiful Offering*)

We give up on obedience when we misunderstand it as a demand for perfection. To be obedient to the instruction of Jesus is a gift back to God. You and I are free to obey, and God has made it easy for us.

I want to make this as simple as possible, so please forgive me if I oversimplify or insult your intelligence. I don't mean to.

God loves you so much.
He made a way through Jesus to save you for eternity.
In the Sermon on the Mount, Jesus gives us living instructions.
God promises to bless that life. He calls it the kingdom life.
The only way to live the kingdom life is through obedience
    to the instructions.
Obedience is the narrow road.
The road leads to God and becoming more like God.
Obedience means that you keep walking toward God. No
    matter what.
All you have to do is keep looking at God.

In your weakness, look for God.

In your failure, find his gaze.

In your imperfection, keep turning in his direction.

You will stay on the narrow path when you have set
your eyes on God.

I believe that if you can understand that obedience is not perfection then you might begin to think, *I can do that. I can hang in there.* If we are on a path, then the goal is to keep moving in the direction of God. Some days we will be sprinting. Some days standing still. Some days lying flat on our faces. But maybe what matters more than anything—sprinting, standing, or fallen—is that we keep our eyes firmly fixed on the One who calls us by name. The One who calls us beautiful. The One who comes to carry us. The One who covers our lack with his grace.

To obey means that you believe God's ways are right. To obey reflects your heart of confidence in his sovereignty. To obey is to rest in his authority as Creator, Redeemer, and Keeper.

God of Second Chances

Sheila Walsh (*I'm Not Wonder Woman / Let Go*)

Consider the story of Cain and Abel: Abel brought the best parts from some of the firstborn of his flock. The LORD accepted Abel and his gift, but he did not accept Cain and his gift. So Cain became very angry and felt rejected. The LORD asked Cain, "Why are you angry? Why do you look so unhappy?"(Gen. 4:4–6 NCV).

At first read, it's hard to understand why Abel's offering was accepted and Cain's was not. Cain worked the land, so it seems logical that he would offer produce of the land. Abel worked with the flocks, so he brought an offering from his flock. However, Abel's gift was from the firstborn lambs—he brought the very best he had to give—but Cain brought a token gift. God always looks beyond the gift to the state of our hearts. What God saw in Cain's heart was a careless gesture compared to the act of worship coming out of his brother's heart. There is also a more far-reaching meaning in that Abel brought a perfect, flawless lamb—a foreshadowing of the coming Christ who would shed his innocent blood in our place. Cain brought the work of his hands, which was not acceptable just as our works have no merit for redemption. We can only come to the Father under the cover of the blood of the Lamb.

But can you see God's mercy in that he gave Cain another chance and a warning? "If you do things well, I will accept you, but if you do not do them well, sin is ready to attack you. Sin wants you, but you must rule over it" (Gen. 4:7 NCV).

Here is one of those crossroad moments. We all have them. We have a moment to choose which path we'll take. Satan can tempt us, but he can't push us onto a path. We choose that for ourselves, and once we do, should we choose the path of giving in to our unbridled emotions, Satan is right there waiting for us.

Cain had a moment to choose as his emotions bubbled under the surface. He was jealous that Abel's offering was accepted the first time and his was not. I'm sure there was defensiveness in his response, too, which is so often present when we know that we have done the wrong thing. That jealousy gave birth to rejection and fueled his anger, and Cain became forever known as the first murderer in human history.

Satan can and will tempt and test us in many ways. What he does not know is how we will respond. We can give in. Or we can look to Jesus, who gave us the perfect responses in his encounters with Satan (in the desert in Matthew 4:1–11): God is my provider. I will not take the easy way out. I will not seek the spectacular; I will seek God's face.

What Satan tempts us with is never what we are really longing for. It may appear to meet a need at the moment, but it will just take us deeper and deeper into the wilderness. Christ's steps keep us close to the heart of God. God has given us his Holy Spirit to guide and direct us. He has given us his Word to be a light to our daily path.

The Blessing of Obedience

Angela Thomas (*A Beautiful Offering*)

I have never regretted obeying Jesus. Not one time. Never. I have thought it was going to be awful. I have feared the outcome of

47

truth-telling and going against the popular vote. But to this day, I have never regretted when I have responded to God in obedience.

Even in your weakness and humanity, God desires to pour his abundance over your obedience. Even when you are broken, even when you don't think you are enough, even when you are persecuted, even then, your obedience brings his blessing. Kingdom abundance means that you have full access to heaven, a hearing with God in a moment's prayer, divine protection, guidance, and the lavish riches of forgiveness, grace, peace, and mercy. When there is abundance, there is more than you need. Enough to give away. Enough for tomorrow. Enough for eternity.

When you and I decide to obey, we have decided to trust that God knows more. Would you humble your heart and choose the narrow gate, follow the narrow road of obedience, and trust that waiting for you is the kingdom abundance of God's blessing?

4

Struggling with Doubt and Fear

The Mustard-Seed Dilemma

Sheila Walsh (*Extraordinary Faith*)

A few years ago I led a women's conference in Pittsboro, North Carolina, and our gracious hostess booked us into a beautiful hotel that was a renovated farmhouse way out in the countryside. My son, Christian, and Martie, who had come along to take care of Christian until we found a new nanny, decided to spend the day at the farm while we were at the church.

At dinner that night, as he was downing his fifth cup of broth, he said, "Mom, did you know that there are bits in the Bible that don't work?"

"No, I didn't," I replied, wondering what was coming. "Which 'bits' are you thinking of?"

"Have you ever read that if you have faith the size of a mustard seed, you could move a mountain?" he asked.

"Yes, I know that passage."

"Well, it doesn't work," he said very seriously. "I tried."

I looked at Martie, hoping she could fill in the blanks. "He tried to move the hills this afternoon," she explained. "We read that passage in his kids' Bible this morning, and he thought that he'd start with the hills in Pittsboro."

"I wanted to move them behind the cows, Mom," he said. "I thought they would look better behind the cows. I told them and told them, but nothing moved! Actually that's not quite true. One of the cows moved, but no hills. I tried all afternoon. It was a disaster!"

We all laughed, but I empathized with Christian. I want my Christian life to be like that too. I want to understand everything. I want to know exactly what God means in every Bible passage, and I want to know that if I will do A, then God will do B. Jesus' words to his disciples are very compelling: "If you have faith as a mustard seed, you will say to this mountain, 'Move from here to there,' and it will move; and nothing will be impossible for you" (Matt. 17:20 NKJV).

That seems pretty straightforward and doable, don't you think? After all, mustard seeds are very small. I had one as a child. It was in a little glass ball that I wore on a chain around my neck. It was a tiny, unimpressive looking offering; it wasn't even a pretty seed or a perfect shape. But I remember as a little girl doing exactly what Christian did and trying to slide the Carrick Hills into the sea. Fortunately for those who love the geography of the west coast of Scotland, my faith did not prevail.

Faith a Size Too Small?

Marilyn Meberg (*God at Your Wits' End*)

When my husband, Ken, was diagnosed with pancreatic cancer, we marshaled all our faith troops together. Scores of people prayed for his healing; we anointed him with oil. In faith we claimed and believed he would experience regenerating life for every cell in his body.

He died fourteen months after his diagnosis.

Was our faith not big enough? Strong enough? Tenacious enough? Would he have lived if we'd found the right "faith person" to pray for him? When our faith failed to move mountains, could someone else's prayers and faith have saved Ken?

My mother's gift of faith and intercessory prayer often ripped the top off seemingly immovable mountains. I knew as a child that though Dad, as a pastor, was the public person, Mom was the faith person. Both my father and I would seek out the encouragement of her gentle but unwavering faith. Early in life my thought about faith was that some have it and some don't, and I believed I fell into the "don't have it" category. For that reason I wanted always to be near my mom's faith center.

When our daughter Joani was born with spina bifida, I was certain she would be healed. The source of my certainty? My mother's powerful prayers of faith. But Joani died when she was fifteen days old. I might have more easily understood her death if I had been the only one praying. But my mother was praying; she was the "right faith person," but . . .

I received a letter last week from a brokenhearted mother whose seventeen-year-old son was heavily involved in the drug scene in their small rural community. Everyone knew everyone. Everyone knew her once-straight-A-student son was blowing his academic scholarship by suddenly failing all his classes.

I was surprised by her question to me. I expected her to ask my thoughts on what might cause this model boy to suddenly veer off onto such a destructive path. Instead, she said, "Faith has never been easy for me, and I know for sure I don't have enough to get my son straightened out. I need to find someone who has a lot of faith. Can you help me?"

I certainly understood her feelings of faith-barrenness and her feeling that someone somewhere has to do the faith thing for her. But do you recognize the faulty thinking not only in her but in me as well? Somehow I, too, felt I had to find a "faith person" for my husband and baby because I feared I wasn't sufficiently faith-endowed. There is nowhere in Scripture that says God has a faith camp where some of his children "have it" and some don't. That thinking is totally unscriptural and a whopper example of faulty thinking. but I'll have to admit this thinking still seeps into my soul from time to time and says, *You need to find someone to believe for you, Marilyn . . . Your faith is shaky. It's too small.*

Changing Our Thinking About Faith

Marilyn Meberg (*God at Your Wits' End*)

Hebrews 11:1–2 says: "What is faith? It is the confident assurance that what we hope for is going to happen. It is the evidence of things we cannot see" (NLT). The fact that we cannot see the evidence does not make our faith blind. Our faith is not in that which is observable. It is placed on God. He is the One who knows what will happen in the future.

Second Corinthians 5:7 says, "We live by believing and not by seeing" (NLT). Believing in whom? God. Not seeing what? The next step. The future. We believe him to be trustworthy with the future . . . with whatever "is going to happen." We trust him with the future because he has a track record of trustworthiness in the past. We look back on our lives and recognize the sovereign orchestration of the events of our lives and say, "That was God's doing!"

Psalm 77:11–12 states, "I recall all you have done, O LORD; I remember your wonderful deeds of long ago. They are constantly in my thoughts. I cannot stop thinking about them" (NLT).

God told Abraham he would father generations of people whose numbers would be greater than the stars one could see in the sky. Abraham believed God, even though if he looked at the evidence, he would see a wife beyond childbearing years, and he would probably question his own potency. Today you and I see the fulfillment of God's promise to Abraham: the Jewish people from Isaac's line and the Arab people from Ishmael's line. That's a pack of people! Abraham did not live long enough to see God's promise totally fulfilled. But *we* see it, and our faith is nourished as a result of seeing the evidence of God's fulfilled promise to Abraham. We think back on those past remembrances of God's promises to his people, and that makes us want to think back on our own remembrances of God's promises to us.

The key to understanding the phrase "assurance that what we hope for is going to happen" is remembering that God has an eternal perspective and we do not. God is not a kindly old grandfather in the sky mindlessly doling out the treats his kids keep asking for. His plan for us is that we come to a deeper understanding of his purpose for us. That understanding is not measured in treats. In fact, that understanding may include experiencing the death of a baby or a husband or suffering some other tragedy that drives us to our wits' end and slams our backs against the wall. These are not "treat experiences," but they are maturity-building experiences. The times I have felt closest to God have been when my requested treats have been withheld. He gave me more than I asked for. I wanted earth stuff; he gave me heaven stuff.

Faith is not a mindless leap into the unknown that's too hard for us to fathom. Faith enables reason to go beyond its human limitations. But faith is not a simple result of reason; it is reason submitting to the truth of Scripture, which is saturated with and enlivened by the Holy Spirit of God. There are mysteries of faith that lie beyond my human understanding, but I believe them because they are rooted in the strength of God's Word. I don't pretend to understand the mystery of God's ways, but Scripture describes God in a way that satisfies my mind. Scripture uses the testimony of eyewitnesses, and that also satisfies my mind.

So what *does* faith require? It requires choosing: choosing to believe. For example, I choose to believe the evidence I see of God in his creation. I can't deny that creative power came from somewhere. I choose to believe it came from God and occurred exactly as described to us in Scripture. Genesis 1:2–3 tells us, "The earth was empty, a formless mass cloaked in darkness. And the Spirit of God was hovering over its surface. Then God said, 'Let there be light,' and there was light" (NLT).

In addition to God the Father of all creation is Jesus, the Son, who "was with God, and he was God. He was in the beginning with God. He created everything there is. Nothing exists that he didn't make. Life itself was in him, and this life gives light to everyone. The light shines through the darkness, and the darkness can never extinguish it" (John 1:1–5 NLT).

I also choose to believe the Word of God, and when I am at my wits' end, I crawl into its pages so my spirit can be enlivened, strengthened, and enabled to believe beyond what I see. The Bible is my faith object. It is crucial to my spiritual balance and my understanding of the degree to which God loves me. I choose to receive into my spirit the words of Psalm 31:7: "I am overcome with joy because of your unfailing love, for you have seen my troubles, and you care about the anguish of my soul" (NLT).

Not only is my soul comforted by the words I read in Scripture but I am also instructed by those words. I learn what faith is. Faith is not as complicated as I have sometimes made it. It is not hard. Quite simply, faith is a gift, and this gift is mine for the taking. It is not a gift I work to be worthy of or can work to achieve. As is true of any gift, I reach out for it. I accept it from the hand of God my Father. Ephesians 2:8 reminds me, "God saved you by his special favor when you believed. And you can't take credit for this; it is a gift from God" (NLT). My part in all this is to accept the gift, to believe in the giver of the gift and then in the gift itself. I trust. I believe. I receive Jesus as Savior. Faith initiates that process.

If faith is not hard, why then does it *seem* hard? Why do we feel at times that we are not walking in faith? Once again, may I suggest, our thinking may be faulty. Our thinking can lead us away from the gift and cause us to muddle about with misperceptions. One such misperception many Christians struggle with is the faulty thought that they don't have as much faith as other people do—that some have it, but they don't.

The fear that our faith is too feeble for Christ to accept is illustrated in Mark 9:24. When Jesus encountered the boy with the demon, the father begged Jesus to heal the boy. Jesus told the father that anything is possible if a person believes. The father's poignant response was, "I do believe; help my unbelief" (NASB). The father seemed to recognize his source of faith was Jesus, but the father also recognized his faith was shaky . . . so he asked for help with it.

We all get into trouble with our faith lives when we forget we ourselves are not the authors or finishers of our faith. Jesus is our total, complete, and forever source of faith. We must know him, rely on him, and accept the fact that all of our strength and competency comes from him. To know that fact and trust in it is to have faith. That is the meaning of Paul's words in Philippians 4:13: "I can do everything through him [Jesus] who gives me strength" (NIV). Jesus said, "Apart from me you can do nothing" (John 15:5 NLT).

Here's the point: God required a sinless, perfect sacrifice. Nowhere do we read that God requires a sinless, perfect *faith*. I can't present a perfect anything. My faith and your faith may sometimes be utterly feeble and weak. But that condition will still connect us to Jesus. It is then that we, too, can cry out, "Lord, I do believe; help my unbelief."

What I love about these clarifying thoughts about faith is that we can quit thinking our prayers will not be valued or heard unless those prayers first rank a high number on the Richter scale of faith. At our most feeble moments, when we are barely able to lift our voices, faith connects us to the One whose ear is ever inclined to the voices of his children.

Now let's apply these thoughts to the situation of the woman who wrote to me about her son who had dropped into the drug scene. She said, "Faith has never been easy for me." The reality is, her faith is carried to the heart of God by the Son of God, no matter how hard faith seems to her or how weak it appears. That's a fact. That may be new thinking, but she can change her thinking and choose to believe what God says in his Word about her faith.

What Is Faith, Anyway?
Sheila Walsh (*Extraordinary Faith*)

After my conversation about faith with my son, Christian, I began to look at the mustard-seed passage in Matthew again. I wanted to help him with his dilemma, and I wanted to glean further understanding for myself.

The word used for "mustard seed" in the New Testament is the Egyptian word *sinapi*. It refers to a plant that begins as a very tiny seed, but if planted in good, fertile soil, it grows to ten or twelve feet. In Matthew 13, Jesus said that the mustard seed, although it is the least of all seeds, grows above all other herbs and offers shelter for the birds of the air. That's quite a bit of progress from such small beginnings.

The image is of something that begins as least likely to succeed, and yet, if placed in the right environment, it will outgrow all the more impressive seeds around it. That doesn't immediately offer me or my son great comfort. Does that mean that I don't have faith as big as the smallest seed of all? If I had this tiny amount of faith, I would be able to tell the mountains to move, but so far, both my son and I are topographically inept. Jesus referred to mustard-seed faith twice in the book of Matthew, once in Mark, and twice in Luke's Gospel. Each instance gives us a different picture of faith.

In Luke 17, Jesus linked faith like a mustard seed not to healing, as in Matthew 17, but to forgiveness. "If your brother sins, rebuke him, and if he repents, forgive him. If he sins against you seven times in a day, and seven times comes back to you and says, 'I repent,' forgive him."

The disciples responded by asking Jesus to give them more faith for this seemingly impossible task. Jesus responded, "If you have faith as small as a mustard seed, you can say to this mulberry tree, 'Be uprooted and planted in the sea,' and it will obey you" (Luke 17:3–4, 6 NIV).

As I read those words in the context of forgiveness, I find it easier to understand. It seems as if Jesus is saying, "Use the faith you have. Don't search for great faith, but if you love me, use what is in you."

"Now faith is the substance of things hoped for, the evidence of things not seen" (Heb. 11:1 NKJV). Throughout the whole canon of Scripture, we have the preceding fifteen words offered to us as the only definition of faith. In other passages we have pictures of those who exhibited faith, what it looks like to break faith, constant exhortations to have faith or stand firm in the faith, to live by faith, rebukes of those with little faith, those who are rewarded because of their faith, and those who will turn away from their faith. But Hebrews 11:1 is the only actual definition of what the content of faith looks like.

In his marvelous book *The Pursuit of God*, A. W. Tozer writes, "In Scripture there is practically no effort made to define faith." In referencing Hebrews 11:1 he writes, "Even there, faith is defined functionally, not philosophically: that is, it is a statement of what faith is in operation, not what it is in essence."[1]

When the writer to the Hebrews offered his definition, he presented it to us as a present reality, not a pursued reality. By that I mean he wrote assuming that the reader already has faith. There is great significance in that. Faith is something to be experienced and exercised, not defined, categorized, and neatly packaged. Tozer shares his experience of faith as "the gaze of a soul upon a saving God." I love that!

As I think of my son standing in a field in North Carolina trying to rearrange the scenery, I am gifted with a clear picture of why we often think as believers that we don't have enough faith. We tend to think:

If we prayed harder . . .

If we prayed in a more compelling tone . . .

If under our breaths we were whispering, "I think I can, I think I can, I think I can . . ."

then we would show enough faith to receive answers to our prayers.

Faith is not wishful thinking or theatrics. Faith is born in us as we fix our eyes on Jesus and as we recognize the fingerprints of God the Father all over our lives.

If you are like me, you have been familiar with the phrase "Fix your eyes on Jesus" for some time, but you may wonder what it means, what it looks like. When I was a teenager I was stumped by Christ's command to pick up my cross every day and follow him. I had no idea how to do that. Did it mean that I should carve up the breakfast table and drag it around the neighborhood? As I studied and prayed, I became convinced that it meant that every time my will crossed God's will, I dragged my will back in line with his. It means doing the things that I know are good and true, whether I feel like it or not. It means setting my face and heart toward heaven just as Jesus did. But what about "Fix your eyes on Jesus"?

I believe that it means that we study how Jesus lived, how he loved, and follow his example. When we find ourselves in a difficult place, we do what he did: we turn to our Father.

Why Is It So Hard to Trust?
Sheila Walsh (*Let Go*)

As believers, trust is foundational to our lives. And yet I think trust is very difficult. What does it mean to trust? Does it mean that we will never be afraid again or that fear will find its proper place; it will have a part in the play but not be the main character? I have been on a journey to understand the connection between fear and trust for a long time. I know that at times in my life I have been crippled by fear, but there has always been this strong call I hear inside my spirit: *Trust me.*

One of the first Scripture passages I ever committed to memory was, "Trust in the LORD with all your heart, and lean not on your own understanding; in all your ways acknowledge Him, and He shall direct your paths" (Prov. 3:5–6 NKJV). As a child, I would ask my mother, "Does that mean I do things that make no sense to me if I believe that God is leading me?" My mom did her best to answer that for an inquisitive twelve-year-old. Children ask very difficult questions! She tried to explain that when I honor God in the choices I make, he will keep me on a straight path. The trouble I had with that was my path didn't always seem straight, even though I was trying to honor God in my choices.

I have gone back to these two verses over and over through the years, and each time I do it's as if there is a little more light cast on the text. "All your heart" seems key to me now. If I trust God with "all my heart," then I leave no part of my heart open to fear. I think for a long time I trusted God with a substantial proportion of my heart but allowed fear to play a bit part. That seemed reasonable to me. After all, we live in a world of people who use us and abuse us; friends can betray us or husbands may leave. God in his wisdom and mercy doesn't always stop the evil that makes its way to our door, so surely fear is part of life on this planet.

Yet evil has always walked this earth since the Fall. Jesus told us over and over again, "Do not be afraid."

To the man whose daughter died before Jesus could make it to his house he said, "Do not be afraid; only believe, and she will be made well" (Luke 8:50 NKJV). To a gathering of his closest friends he said, "My friends, do not be afraid of those who kill the body, and after that have no more that they can do" (Luke 12:4 NKJV). From Genesis to Revelation, there is a call from God the Father and Christ his Son—trust me; don't be afraid!

I used to think that when God said if I trust him, he would make my path straight, it meant without bumps or curves. Now I believe that it means my path is leading me home no matter how crooked it looks. The other major change is a deeper understanding of who I am being asked to trust. The longer I walk with my Father, the easier it is for me to trust him. I will not always like where he takes me but if it's where he's going, then I'm going too. That's my prayer every morning now: "Father, today I place my hand in your hand. Wherever you are going, I'm coming with you. I won't always understand, but I trust your heart. I trust your love."

I think another part of the process began when I took a fresh look at Jesus' mother, Mary, in what had to be the worst moment of her life. Even for Mary, trust had its own learning curve. She discovered there was a calling on her life that was far greater than her calling as a mother. It was the calling to be a follower of her son, Jesus, the Christ. She had to let go of what she cherished more than her own life to embrace a higher calling.

Even as Jesus hung on the cross in an agony of soul and spirit, he looked down and saw his mother. How often had he looked into those eyes as a child and known such love? How often had she loved him, cherished him, sung to him, and tenderly wiped blood from his knee when he fell running across the yard to tell her some news? What mother could bear to see her firstborn son executed in such a barbaric way, mocked and tortured? What had her trust in God gained her?

You might be tempted to ask why this account of what happened to Mary was so liberating for me. I think it's because Jesus took what Mary believed about herself and showed her another path. She got the bigger picture. She had lost her husband and watched men torture and kill her firstborn son, so she knew pain and loss and the fear that her trust had been betrayed. But no one could touch who she was. When we see her last in the Scriptures, she is waiting with the other disciples for the promise of the Holy Spirit— she is going about her Father's business. She had known the joy of marriage and motherhood, but in the end her greatest call was to trust—as a disciple of Jesus Christ.

Dear reader, that means wherever you are in your life right now, the joy and purpose that Mary knew is within your grasp. You don't have to be afraid of what might happen to you, to your family, to your children, to your careers. You don't have to live in mistrust because of what happened to you in the past. If you can begin to grasp the magnitude of what Jesus offers, there will be peace *now*, in the midst of life.

I do not for one moment want to minimize the pain of what your life has brought you—or what might come. All I'm saying is there is a Rock we have been invited to build our lives on, and this Rock cannot be shaken. What Mary saw in the eyes of her son as he was dying was not fear or hatred—it was love. That is the greatest mystery and gift of all. We have not been put on some kind of spiritual endurance course to see if we can make it all the way home; rather, we have been placed on a path and asked to walk beside the love of our lives. If you are in a good marriage, I celebrate that with you even as I remind you that God's love is far greater. If you find yourself in a place of loss or disappointment, I long to remind you that you are loved more than you would ever have the wisdom to ask for.

This is the key for me: we are loved by the One who is love. We are loved by the One who has overcome the enemy. We are loved by the One who says, *Trust me*.

Growing in Faith
Marilyn Meberg (*God at Your Wits' End*)

Paul said in Romans 10:17 that faith comes from hearing the Word of God. I grow, you grow, everyone grows by studying the Word of God. The Bible is our faith object. Our faith grows as we study it. Romans 10 (vv. 8–13) is translated in *The Message* Bible this way:

> It's the word of faith that welcomes God to go to work and set things right for us. This is the core of our preaching. Say the welcoming word to God—"Jesus is my Master"—embracing,

body and soul, God's work of doing in us what he did in raising Jesus from the dead. That's it. You're not "doing" anything; you're simply calling out to God, trusting him to do it for you. That's salvation. With your whole being you embrace God setting things right, and then you say it, right out loud: "God has set everything right between him and me!" Scripture reassures us "No one who trusts God like this—heart and soul—will ever regret it. . . . Everyone who calls, 'Help, God!' gets help."

What fantastic encouragement these words from Scripture provide. Forgive me, but I'm going to throw out a formula I see in this Romans passage:

- I say the words "Help, God."
- I trust him to help me.
- I remember I'm not doing anything; I'm calling out to God and trusting him to do it for me.

Does this sound too easy? Too passive? Too laid back in my hammock and munching Milk Duds while God works? It is not passive at all, in that God not only invites our participation as he builds our faith lives, but also he requires it. You try lying back in your hammock, and he'll tip you out of it. You are in a loving partnership, but he's in charge. I first say the words, then I trust God with my growth, and he takes over. But he takes me with him.

So what about the hurting mother with the son involved in drugs? These were my suggestions to her:

- Begin changing your thinking from *I'm not good at faith* to *Jesus gave me faith when I received him.*
- Begin thinking, *My words are always, always presented lovingly to the Father, who always, always hears them.*
- Know that your new thinking takes you to Jesus-inspired faith: *I believe, Lord; help me.*
- Study his Word every day.
- Talk to him daily in prayer if only by saying his name: "Jesus, Jesus, Jesus." There is more power in that name than in any word in any language in the universe.
- Memorize Psalm 34:17 and say it out aloud over and over: "The LORD hears his people when they call to him for help. He rescues them from all their troubles" (NLT).

I also told her, "The God of the universe knows your son. He sees your son, and he cares for your son. Trust God to do what God plans to do. It may not be in your timing or your way, but when it is God's way the promise is, 'We know that God causes everything to work together for the good of those who love God and are called according to his purpose for them'" (Rom. 8:28 NLT).

Feeling as if We'll Never Measure Up

Driven Christian Girls

Tammy Maltby (*Confessions of a Good Christian Girl*)

My friend Donna is beautiful. And not just everyday beautiful. I'm talking supermodel gorgeous—tall, slim, amazing blue eyes, exotic cheekbones, a dazzling smile. She actually worked as a model at one point in her life. Donna is successful, too, with a professional background in public relations and a new position as an analyst for a wireless broadband research firm. On the side, she's an independent consultant for a company that sells high-end clothing at home parties, which means she dresses extremely well.

Donna lives with her husband and three little girls in a lovely house in a nice neighborhood with a spectacular view of the mountains. She's a dedicated Christian, a loving and committed wife and mother, a talented musician, a loyal friend. In fact, if you met Donna, you'd be convinced she has it all—high energy, loads of talent, a sweet personality. She is truly an impressive woman. You'd never guess she struggles every day with the same issue that plagues so many good Christian girls I know . . . the feeling of never quite measuring up.

But she does struggle, every day of her life. No matter how hard she works—and she works very hard—she's haunted by the suspicion that she's doing her life all wrong. On the job, she second-guesses herself on her decision to leave her PR career. She worries that her skills aren't adequate to be a top achiever in her new field. (She has a history of quitting any pursuit where she can't excel.) She worries that she and her husband don't make enough money but also wonders if she's cheating her kids by not being a stay-at-home mom and not volunteering at their school more often. Whether she stays up late to bake cookies for a classroom party or grabs a box from the grocery store, she fears she's shortchanging someone or being judged by someone else.

At church, Donna worries about turning down an invitation to perform in a church musical. At home, though she prays every morning, she kicks herself for not studying or reading the Bible more. In the neighborhood, she compares herself to the full-time moms and the women working outside the home who have household help.

She's sure they're checking out her house and yard and children and her activities and judging her for her shortcomings.

Donna admits she's "hyper-driven." She also admits she's weary of trying so hard and that her constant striving causes conflict with her family and friends. She knows she needs to learn to "rest in the Lord," and with counseling and lots of prayer she's learning to relax a little. But even then, she worries that she's not relaxing enough . . .

Does any of this sound familiar?

If you're a good Christian girl, I'm almost certain it does. Because feeling inadequate may not be as dramatic as being abused or having an addiction, but it can be fully as painful. And it's definitely more pervasive. Sometimes it seems like everyone I know suffers from some variation of this mind-set. I see it in the frustrated tears of women who come to hear me speak. I hear it in the weary voices of women I overhear in the coffee shop and of the friends who join me there. I also feel it in my own heart, especially when other painful issues of my life press in on me.

That's when I start comparing myself with the woman next door. Or thinking I need a new outfit for the occasion I'm going to. Or feeling guilty for flipping through a magazine when I could be starting dinner or reading my Bible. Or telling myself I need to be much more productive in all my work. Or reminding myself that one child or another needs more attention and time with me.

And yes, there's a reason Donna and I are friends. We're sisters in our insecurities, our restlessness, our sense that something might fall apart if we ever truly relaxed. (Given the way we've set up our lives, it might!) And we're like so many women I know. Women who wrestle with a constant sense of being inadequate or judged or not measuring up. And carry a burden of guilt because of our failures and inadequacies. And wear ourselves out with the effort of constantly improving ourselves—or feeling we're expected to.

We're both good Christian girls, of course. That's part of the problem. We want to be good Christian girls. We also want to be good wives and irresistible lovers and great moms and loving daughters and successful businesswomen and powerful prayer partners and loyal friends. We're programmed to meet needs and fulfill expectations, and we try so very hard to do just that. But we're still bombarded with messages from the inside and the outside that tell us we're just not _____ enough. (You fill in the blank!)

The specifics vary, but that constant familiar litany keeps on sounding in our ears, reminding us:

We've got to work harder.
And do better.
And keep trying.
And reach for excellence.
And meet others' needs and expectations.
And live up to our own high standards.
And not give up, no matter what.

I don't know about you, but just thinking about it makes me tired. Living it is enough to make me throw up my hands.

The Perfect Package

Lisa Whittle (*Behind Those Eyes*)

The *perfect package* is the woman who knows it all, sees it all, does it all, whips it up for dinner, and sells it for a profit. (You know, she's the one you and I are intimidated and annoyed by.) She dresses impeccably, has money to burn, and sews her own curtains. But she calls them *window treatments* since she knows the importance of semantics. She manages her household, stays in touch with her friends, organizes neighborhood get-togethers, and doesn't break a sweat. She returns phone calls promptly, decorates her home professionally, and never misses her boss's birthday. She is overworked yet never stressed. She has a Colgate smile and a size 4 body. She finds time to scrapbook, run marathons, and serve on the town council. She is the personification of a perfect package.

By the way, she may or may not be married. The perfect package is different from the perfect wife or perfect mom while they share many of the same characteristics. Seeking perfection in outward appearance is certainly one of them. The perfect package is focused on making her outside look better by any and every means necessary, which may include tweaking, nipping, tucking, pulling, stretching, bleaching, manicuring, lasering, zapping, and camouflaging.

But perfect packages don't stop there. Since they are constantly researching how to present perfection to others, they are fully aware of their need to be *evolved* on the inside. Their bookshelves are lined with self-help books. They TiVo pop psychologists and listen to lectures on "Ten Days to a Better You." The perfect package first needs to *feel* perfect in order for her to sell others on it. And it's become a full-time job. Though we typically think of Ms. Perfection as one of our peers, being programmed to present oneself as a perfect package can start at a very early age.

Young or more mature, single or married, childless or a mother of multiples, Ms. Perfection is easily impersonated by women across the country. We want to be the perfect wife, perfect mother, and perfect woman all wrapped up in a perfect package. Even though we know in our hearts that it's not possible, we still strive for perfection. And it is killing our souls and hearts in the process.

The People Who Judge Us
Tammy Maltby (*Confessions of a Good Christian Girl*)

As the mother of young women, I often cringe at the "not enough" messages our culture sends them. An article in the *San Francisco Chronicle* reported that girls are more stressed than ever about their weight, grades, and sex, according to three new studies by Girls Inc. Calling it the "supergirl dilemma," researchers found that girls still feel pressure to please everyone and look perfect while also trying to seize opportunities their grandmothers might not have had, such as attending college and pursuing careers.

One girl said, "The problem is I can never be thin enough, I can never be pretty enough, and I can never be good enough" . . .

Nationally, 60 percent of girls reported that they often feel stressed, and 33 percent of girls said they often feel sad and unhappy. Even in elementary school, nearly half of respondents said they feel stressed.[1]

Who knows how many of those "stressed" children and teenagers will end up being tomorrow's frantic and driven Christian women?

But it's not just a generalized "out there" culture that pressures girls and women to do better and better, to meet impossible standards. Specific people in our life—influenced by the culture as well and by their own insecurities and warped perceptions—set the "enough" bar impossibly high. The people in our past—peers, siblings, and especially our parents—wield an especially powerful influence. What they say to us and the way they treat us during childhood and adolescence tend to stick deep in our minds.

The voices of our past can echo loudly in our hearts and minds, but people in our present fuel our "not enough" feelings as well. Competitive colleagues and bosses, critical (older) parents and siblings, high-achieving friends and neighbors and school parents, pastors and church friends, even our own husbands and children dish out the message that we've got to try harder to be loved and accepted.

It's easy enough—and accurate enough—to blame our drivenness, our "not enough" mentality, on outside forces such as culture and the expectations of others. It really isn't "all in our head." People do judge us. Society judges us. Other Christians judge us, and often quite harshly.

At the same time, if we're really honest, we driven Christian girls will have to admit that often the person who puts the biggest "not enough" pressure on us is . . . us.

We experience rejection and resolve to be nicer so it won't happen again. We fall on our face and pick ourselves up and vow to run faster next time. We look at our successful friends and neighbors and colleagues and conclude we're woefully inadequate and need to try harder. We grow up in chaos and feel the need to tighten our grip. We read the Bible (parts of it) and decide we'd better get busy winning people to Christ.

But what's really driving us, much of the time, is not what happened to us or what other people or even God expects of us. What's driving us is what we think has happened or is expected. Or, more to the point, what we think will ease our pain or boost our egos or make us feel better. It's not always a conscious process. It's hard to sort out our own motivations and easy to get confused about what has happened to us and what it means. Our faulty thinking and mistaken conclusions fuel our sense of inadequacy.

So before we know it, we're huffing and puffing through life. Working longer hours. Juggling priorities and scheduling every minute and getting up early and staying up late. Doing everything we can to measure up to our own view of what we're supposed to accomplish. Worrying we still won't be able to get it all done.

And interestingly enough, we often do very well . . . for a while. We do good work. We help others. Our efforts seem to bring glory to God and bring us confidence and a healthy sense of accomplishment—until we finally run head first into our own limitations. Then we get sick from the stress. Or we develop addictions and compulsions, obsessing with feeling better about ourselves, leaning on substances like alcohol or tobacco or caffeine to give us a boost and help us keep at it. We may throw up our hands and give up . . . or grow depressed . . . or stop correcting our faults and call that "accepting ourselves." We may demand that the world adjust to us and grow bitter and frustrated when it doesn't. Or pretend to be good enough, sacrificing honesty in the interest of cleaning up well and looking happy.

The Truth About Our Inadequacies

Tammy Maltby (*Confessions of a Good Christian Girl*)

Actually, most of us do all of the above at one time or the other—or at the same time—in different areas of our lives. And no matter which response we choose, the seeds of "not enough" grow into a bitter harvest. We may end up weary and frustrated. Resentful of others' needs and expectations. Judgmental of their weaknesses. Envious of their possessions or talents. We may be angry with God (whether we know it or not) for not giving us what we want. Angry with ourselves and sure that our inadequacies are to blame for the bad things that have happened to us. So caught up in our own problems that we have trouble seeing anybody else. And unable to appreciate or even see the abundant blessings God has laced through our lives.

And "enough" still remains a moving target . . . always out
there ahead of us.

Always out of reach.

Because the truth is we will *never* be enough.

But in the economy of God, "not enough" is not really an issue.
What is an issue is our skewed thinking about who we are and
what's expected of us—our stubborn insistence on more, more,
more. We let the contradictory messages of culture and the unhappy
voices of people we know and our own inclinations turn our "not
enough" reality into frantic attempts at self-sufficiency.

And that's where we really get ourselves in trouble.

Because that's where "not enough" and "try harder" start sounding a lot like sin.

Sinful Drivenness

Tammy Maltby (*Confessions of a Good Christian Girl*)

I'm not saying it's a sin to feel inadequate or even to feel driven. I
don't think any feeling is a sin—because we don't really have control over how we feel. (We do have control over how we respond to
our feelings, but that's a different issue.) I certainly don't believe
it's a sin to work hard or improve ourselves.

There's nothing inherently wrong with losing weight or wearing makeup or even having a tummy tuck. I generally applaud

women who make a success of their businesses or put a lot of effort into being a good mom or feel compelled to throw themselves into Christian service. Jesus never called us to be lazy, ineffective slobs! At the same time, drivenness is a danger issue. It's very easy for "not enough" to shift into sinful thinking and "try harder" to morph into sinful behavior.

Pride is a common downfall for driven Christian girls, for example. We tell ourselves we just have high standards, but secretly we're trying to be better than everyone else. Or we take on more responsibility because we secretly feel that we should be in charge. "I'm never enough" can really translate into "It's all about me— I'm responsible for everything that happens in the world."

And drivenness easily morphs into hypocrisy and self-righteousness, the sins that Jesus judged most harshly. The more we push ourselves toward our own view of perfection, the harder we try to be enough on our own, the more likely we are to either pretend that all is well when it isn't or to point our fingers at others' inadequacies.

Have you ever thought that drivenness can be a form of lust? How many times do we tell ourselves "I'm not enough" when what we really mean is "I want more"? That desire for more and more of a good thing is a built-in part of our sinful nature. So is the kind of self-deceit that tries to cover the desire with a more socially accept-able insecurity.

In the same way, "I'm not enough" thinking can hide a very basic failure of faith—what we're really feeling is "God is not enough for me" or "I can't depend on God." Our striving may reflect our perpetual dissatisfaction with what we have been given and our desire for different blessings than what God has chosen to bestow.

Whenever good Christian girls are driven and striving and hurting and unhappy, I think it's fair to assume that sin is inevitably involved. But that shouldn't surprise us. As I've mentioned again and again, we live in a fallen world. That means we will sin, and we will be sinned against, and all this sin is likely to fuel our "not enough" drivenness. But driven Christian girls who are not enough have Jesus . . . who is enough.

That really does make all the difference. Or at least it gives us a place to start.

What We Really Need

Tammy Maltby (*Confessions of a Good Christian Girl*)

You see, the big question for driven Christian girls is not whether God can help us. We know he can—we're good Christian girls, remember? We know God forgives our sins and saves our souls. We've tasted his goodness, experienced his grace. What we haven't been able to do is open ourselves to his rest. We can't seem to let go of our "not enough" fears and desires that keep us so insecure and exhausted.

Most of us, I'd guess, have told ourselves to lighten up, only to fall back into our old driven thinking. We've tried and failed to heed the message of Psalm 37:7 and Matthew 11:28—to rest in the Lord and to come to him for rest. We've accepted the good news that Jesus is all we need, and we really believe that. But we can't seem to stop feeling driven and needy.

> So we wonder if we need therapy. (That's a possibility. I strongly encourage broken people to seek out Christian therapy . . . it has literally changed my life.)
> Or in-depth Bible study. (That's always a good idea.)
> Or prayer and meditation. (It's a powerful source of help.)
> Or the support of friends, pastors, and teachers. (Definitely a must—because we're not enough, remember?)

But in the long run, the Lord's word of grace to those of us who are harried and hassled and driven and striving, those of us who can't shake the voice of "I'm not enough," starts with the word he gave to another harried and hassled and driven woman who happened to be one of his favorite people—Martha of Bethany. The one who fussed and fretted about throwing a perfect dinner party for Jesus and his friends and got upset because her sister, Mary, didn't help.

I've given a lot of dinner parties, and I can picture the scene so clearly. There's Martha ladling sauce into a bowl or folding a cloth for the bread basket, assuming her sister is right there with her. She says something like, "Could you bring me the basket from the window ledge?" No answer. So she turns around, realizes she's alone, and blows her top. She goes storming into the room where Jesus sits, disciples all around him, Mary at his feet. And the sight of them all just sitting there just makes things worse.

"Lord," she whines, "I'm doing all this stuff to make you welcome, and Mary's just sitting there. Don't you care? Make her come help me!"

I've always wondered what Mary did at that moment. Maybe she felt guilty and started to get up. Maybe she just rolled her eyes and looked at Jesus with an expression that said, *My crazy sister is at it again*. Maybe she went over and hugged Martha because she knew the pain that drove her sibling to be such a perfectionist.

We don't know what Mary did. We just know what Jesus said—and his word for us driven Christian girls is just as gentle, just as full of grace as his words to Martha that day.

"Martha, Martha," he told her softly, "You are worried and concerned with many things, but only one thing is needed."

The Voice to Listen To

Tammy Maltby (*Confessions of a Good Christian Girl*)

"Only one thing." I hope those words were enough to calm Martha's driven heart, to slow her hands, to change her perspective. (They help me a lot when I can wrap my mind around them.) I hope she heard what Jesus was really saying, which was not, "Don't serve, don't work, don't try," but, "First things first."

What he was telling her, with exquisite love and tenderness, was, "You need me most of all. And here I am—so you can relax!"

Isn't that the word that all of us need to hear, the word that can not only calm our hearts but also, over time, change them?

We are worried about so many things. So much occupies our attention and drives us to work and work, try and try again, or give up in frustration. So many voices conspire to tell us that we're not up to snuff, that our efforts are insufficient, that we ought to be ashamed because something serious is wrong with us. So many voices urge us to work harder, try harder, get busier, not let up . . . because if we ever did, everything might fall apart.

But in the midst of it all, there's just one thing we need to do. We need to put down our spoons and dishrags and planners and to-do lists and focus in on the One who loves us best. The One who whispers, *Listen to me first. Not to the expectations of others. Not to the pain from your past or your fears of the future. Let my voice be the one that guides you. Let me show you what it means to sit at my feet and rest.*

For as we choose to focus on him . . . to keep listening for his voice . . . he starts changing the way we look at ourselves and him. And as that happens, we start to settle down. Our driven impatience gives way to contentment. (Yes, it really can happen.) Our dissatisfaction relaxes into gratitude. It's all part of what Paul calls the renewing of our minds (Rom. 12:2). We think differently. Our perspective changes. And gradually we realize that we're different, less driven people.

Practically speaking, it happens as we set aside time to come to him. As we talk to him over the course of the day. As we listen to him in his Word and the silence of our hearts. As we consciously choose to trust him. To practice waiting for his timing. And deliberately giving thanks for his blessings.

But I'm not telling you the way to get over your drivenness and compulsiveness is to work harder on prayer and Bible study, to try more diligently to be content and thankful. That would be a typical driven Christian girl response—to hear just another "not enough" message on top of all the other issues. And that's not what Jesus is saying. It's not what he asks of us.

What he wants is our attention. Our listening ears. Our willingness to turn to him, to expose our thoughts and feelings to his influence. And most of all, to open our hearts to the truth of what God thinks about us.

We Are Completely Loved

Lisa Whittle (*Behind Those Eyes*)

God already knows that he accepts us just as we are . . . with all of our failures and faults and insecurities, but he wants *us* to know that—to *really* know that. He's written us love letter after love letter in his Holy Word, the Bible, but we still sometimes have a hard time grasping the fact that we are accepted totally . . . completely, truly, and 100 percent accepted. Though he has proven to us time and again that even when we mess up he doesn't stop loving and accepting us, we still seek his approval.

It's hard for most if not all of us to realize that God's acceptance of us is not like the acceptance (or lack thereof) we get from our worldly relationships. The truth is we never totally feel accepted every day by anyone on this earth, even the people who love and care for us the very most. We often feel judged and compromised by the people around us, and we just can't seem to shake the feeling that God also somehow reserves his opinion of us, depending upon how we behave or what we say and do. We fear that the jury may be still out about us, and the Judge hasn't had his final say.

The depth of God's love for us is hard to comprehend. So are the height, the width, and the breadth of his love. Our human minds will not allow us to process the greatness of the love of our Father because we are programmed by the world's view of love, which has great limitations. The handbook of worldly love outlines for us some guidelines we must follow in order to ever find it. Things like, *Remember that love is just a feeling . . . If you love someone, let him go . . . Recognize that you are the biggest love of your own life* . . . Nice captions for greeting cards but hardly the gospel truth.

How God Sees Us

Tammy Maltby (*Confessions of a Good Christian Girl*)

The entire message of the Bible, as I see it, has to do with how God sees us. And the Bible has both good news and bad news about that.

The truth is we're not enough . . . because we're incomplete and imperfect and weak.

Because we're sinful and rebellious.

Because we're supposed to work together and we just can't get along.

Because we need God desperately and we forget that reality on an hourly basis.

We're so inadequate, in fact, that it's downright pitiful. And that's the bad news.

But here's the good news—and it's amazingly good. Even in the midst of our inadequate, lying, sinning reality, God loves us passionately. Tenderly. Enthusiastically. With a Father's care and tenderness. He sees so much potential. He wants so much for us. For thousands of years he's been pursuing us, making it possible for us to draw near to him. He even sent his Son to save us—not because of our efforts, but simply because we're his.

That's hard to understand, I know. Believe me—I know! I still struggle with my compulsive, workaholic tendencies. I still wrestle with the pain my inadequacies cause me and those I love. I'm still ashamed to be not enough, and I keep bustling around to rectify the situation when what I really need to be doing is turning to Jesus. But I'm gradually beginning to understand. God's grace is teaching me.

Our inadequacies, our failures, our "not enough" issues are simply beside the point when it comes to the Father's love.

Yes, he has his standards.

Yes, he wants to help us be more like him.

Yes, he has work for us all to do, and I believe he delights in our hard work and creativity when it's combined with obedience and honest truth.

But even if we never did a thing, our Father would still love us. He continues to love us when we fail, when we run from him, when our thinking is skewed and our intentions are all wrong. Even when we persist in thinking we can never be enough through our own efforts. We must sound so silly as we huff and puff and whine and wheeze and try harder and harder and wallow in our worries. But if we let him, he can love us back to sanity. He'll give us rest. Even better, he'll give us peace.

Remember what Jesus told the woman with the issue of blood?

He told her to go in peace. He said the same thing to the Luke 7 woman, the notorious sinner who anointed his feet with perfume.

And I believe that's his crowning word for us good Christian girls who try and try and still don't feel like we're enough.

It means "nothing missing, nothing broken."

It means being whole, enough, sufficient. It means being able to relax, not strive, because we're so confident that we're loved. It means doing all our work with a changed perception. An attitude of grateful, peaceful confidence.

Because we're his children.

And because, to him, we are never anything less than beloved.

Lean In

Angela Thomas (*A Beautiful Offering*)

God sees that it's just you. And he loves it when you lean into him with everything you have and everything you don't have and trust. That's the kind of heart he's happy to bless.

Do you long to hear the compassionate grace of God today? Do you need a break from trying so hard and always coming up short? Would it soothe your soul to quit whining about your weakness and shout, "I need a Savior!"? 'Cause when you get it, when it is settled in your heart that you will never be enough, then the glory of God comes into focus.

You see him.

Maybe for the first time, you see his splendor in light of who you are.

6

Living Life
on Our Terms

The Danger in Disappointment

Paula Rinehart (*Better Than My Dreams*)

Not everyone is afflicted with great expectations.

Many of us secretly believe that the safest path is the one where our hearts are kept on a tight leash. If we don't want much . . . we are seldom disappointed. A short wish list makes for an easier life— or so it seems. No one would accuse us of harboring great expectations. At some invisible place we don't even remember, we decided to aim low and to retreat from the risky places where our hearts might take a painful hit or two. We get good at settling. It's a familiar tale—one that thousands of us live—and if folks knew our real story, they would understand why.

When my daughter Allison was riding the roller coaster of hoping for a child and yet suffering through repeated miscarriages, I saw this temptation up close. We had many conversations about hope and expectation. Every empty month that rolled by meant another round of disappointment—and the inclination to despair. "You can't let go of hope, honey, just because you are disappointed," I would say. "You can't retreat into a cocoon of resignation."

Allison's response voiced what all of us have felt at some point. "But, Mom, it hurts to hope."

Do you know what she means? It takes such courage to stay awake to possibility—to keep bringing a hungry heart back to God, over and over, until he says it's time to let go. It takes faith to believe that if God says no to a good dream . . . it means God is up to something that will, eventually, have his glory written all over it. Indeed, it can hurt to hope.

Some of us live with chronically low expectations because our energy is going elsewhere. We are busy patrolling the edges of our lives, fending off potential threats, managing our fears. We stopped dreaming long ago. If something tragic or repeatedly painful has happened in a woman's past, she can get stuck in the mode of merely protecting herself—but not really living and trusting God. All that energy goes into living as a border patrol.

The danger in our lives is not that we'll be disappointed if we

let our hearts off the leash—if we really step out there on the playing field and see where God takes us. The real thing to fear is that
we'll try to manage disappointment on our own.

You can feel the way the enemy spots each of us in our most
vulnerable moments and whispers in our ears something that seems
true in isolation. *It's just you, honey, up against a cold, cruel world,
and God is nowhere to be found. You have to make the best of it. Alone.
You are all alone.*

So we bury our hearts in the backyard somewhere. We bundle
up our angst and anxiety, our fear and our loss, into a neat package
and *get on with it.* What dies on the inside, though, is some of the
hope and expectation meant to fuel the journey. And we come to
conclusions about God that are tragically inaccurate.

Struggling with God
Paula Rinehart (*Better Than My Dreams*)

The struggle itself is not some alien condition—as though we lost
our spot on the victory train of spiritual success stories. The struggle is part of the relationship. It's what makes for intimacy.

It's important to realize that wrestling through disappointment
with God has a rich tradition in the Bible. Think of how David
struggled with God as he hid out in caves and wondered aloud if,
perhaps, God had forgotten him (see Psalm 13). Or Jeremiah, who
admitted that he felt like God had driven him into darkness and

made him live there. He survived by reminding himself of truth, in words we have come to love:

> The Lord's lovingkindnesses indeed never cease,
>> For His compassions never fail.
> They are new every morning;
>> Great is Your faithfulness.
> (Lam. 3:22–23 NASB)

When Jesus returned to the Father, he spoke words that touch the deepest emotional needs of our hearts: "I will come again . . . that where I am, there you may be also" (John 14:3 NASB). He is coming to take us home. And *home* is truly what we long for. In between now and then, however, we are following a trail of faith to a place we have not gone, led by Someone we have not met—in precise terms. Of course, we struggle to find our way.

On an emotional plane, there are two extremes on a continuum we call hope. We can live in a place of entitlement, with expectations that really belong in heaven. But the other possibility, and the one we've been exploring here, is just as ominous—that of settling. Just settling for whatever comes and asking for little else. Both extremes will pull you away from the rich opportunity of being on a journey with God and finding life in knowing—really knowing—him.

As Jesus said,

> *Ask* and it will be given to you; *seek* and you will find; *knock* and the door will be opened to you. (Matt. 7:7 NIV; emphasis added)

Notice how active those words are: *ask, seek,* and *knock.* Think of the way Jacob wrestled with God and God blessed his life—or the way David poured out his heart to the Lord (see Genesis 32; Psalm 32). There is some kind of truly interactive process when you bring the real desires of your heart to God and he reshapes your inner being. This journey you are on with God has all the pulls and tugs, ebbs and flows of a true relationship.

The Longing for Something More
Paula Rinehart (*Better Than My Dreams*)

The angst of longing for something more is what makes us human— and what pulls us to God. He asks us to let him shape our desires—to purify and refine and hone them like sharp arrows. And then he gives the capacity to carry that hope within us until the time is right. Until his time is right.

The only way to keep your heart alive in the face of all that life throws your way is to decide that there are worse things than being disappointed. Our extraordinary efforts to keep from being hurt are mostly a waste of energy. Unfortunately, in a fallen world, disappointment is a given. It's more like a fact of life.

The really important part is where we go with an aching heart. The first time the totally unexpected happened in my life and I lost dreams and relationships that seemed irretrievable, I responded like many women do—I retreated into a quiet cocoon on the inside where no one could reach me. Not even God. And while I showed up where I needed to and kept the mechanics of a family going, I knew I was playing a role. I just couldn't name what was happening in me. For the first time ever, I found dust gathering on my Bible and the conversation with God shut down from my end.

One morning before daybreak, I woke up early and a bit irritated that I was losing sleep on such a regular basis. As I lay there, I became aware of the presence of Jesus, sitting, as it were, at the foot of my bed. It was so real that I instinctively looked for the indention in the mattress. I had no category for this sort of experience, so it caught me unaware.

Before I could think further, though, very clearly and very simply words formed in my mind, so distinct they might as well have been audible.

You are angry.

I had to think about that for a minute. Southern women don't get angry—or at least, we often don't know it if we are.

Hmm, I said to myself, *maybe that's it; maybe I am angry*—rather surprised to be given a label for this shutdown place in which I was living.

Immediately, his response came as surely as if the words were spoken. *Yes, you are angry . . . and if you'll let me walk with you through that, I'll bring you out the other side.*

I lay there and watched the sun come up, tears trickling down my face. I would never have believed that Jesus would meet me in such a way—or at such a messy, confused time in my life. I was amazed by his kindness. I could not—at that point—have let another living soul see the doubts and questions stirring in me and yet, somehow, God came after me in this dark place. He offered to bring me out the other side of whatever this was, and I knew I could not get there on my own.

Those small moments with God became a huge hinge in my life. Anger is often the face of loss and disappointment, like a doorway you have to go through to get to the real stuff. It's a hard scab on some wound in your heart that must be melted so the tender, vulnerable parts of you can know his touch.

Perhaps the richest part of this journey is discovering that God is not put off by a heart in bad need of repair. He, indeed, sits at the foot of our beds, waiting for us to recognize his presence where we least expect.

How Did I Forget?

Angela Thomas (*A Beautiful Offering*)

Once upon a time there was a woman (that would be me) who sometimes wished she was still a little girl (the me I used to be). This little girl in the grown woman's body remembers when she never worried about anything. She didn't worry about being safe at night or what to make for dinner. She never gave one thought to paying a bill or buying groceries or college funds. She just skipped along, trusting the people who had always been trustworthy. Eventually, she met God and began to trust him just the same. That little girl had a cushy life and mushy love and a great, big God whom she never doubted.

Then one day the grown-up little girl realized that she was on a journey and everyone else was on a journey too. We take a certain path, and then we're forced to accept the consequences and surprises that come to us on the way. Sometimes the road makes a quick turn we hadn't planned for. Sometimes there are accidents or mistakes and the journey is delayed. Sometimes we fall down and stay down and give up on ever completing the distance. And then sometimes attackers ambush our lives or pilfer our dreams or slip away into the night with our hearts.

On the journey, there are things that we need to survive and there are things that we desire to enjoy. And the grown-up little girl learned to worry about the things she thought she needed and the path that was in front of her and the would-be thieves hiding in the dark. The grown-up little girl came to believe that she was making this trip all alone. And she became so very afraid of the journey. She was afraid that her needs would not be met. And she was afraid that she'd never embrace her desires. And she was afraid that somebody or some awful thing would come along and take her life too soon. It seemed as though everyone she met on the journey was worried and filled with anxiety too.

Eventually, she heard about a place in the road up ahead. Evidently the path wasn't clear, and rumor had it that some of the road had washed away. She heard travelers murmuring that there was a bridge impossible to cross. Others had posted signs that read,

"Turn Back, Road Closed, Bridge Out." And the grown-up little girl didn't know what to do. So she sat down to retrace her steps.

She knew that she belonged to God and this journey had been given to her by him. He called this adventure a gift, and he promised to provide all she would need. When she looked back through the maps of her heart, she realized the great distance she had already come with God. He had overseen every step, provided every need, and carried every burden. In fact, she had never been alone for a minute. And she wondered why she had forgotten so easily and given herself over to fear.

So, when the grown-up little girl had retraced the steps of God's presence in her life and after she remembered that he had always provided, then she turned her heart in the direction of the kingdom and fixed her eyes on the Author and Perfecter of this faith journey. She gathered the ones she loved and held them close and whispered into their ears, "Not to worry. I don't know how I forgot, but we belong to God. This journey is his. We are going to walk toward the sound of his voice. And when the path seems impossible and the way is unclear, then we shall expect a bridge."

Seek First and Watch God Provide

Angela Thomas (*A Beautiful Offering*)

I doubt that my mama remembers, but when I was in college she wrote a letter to me, promising that one day I'd be loved by a man. She said that obviously the man who could love me wasn't ready. God still had him in training. I remember her writing that "he is waiting in the wings, learning his lines, and will join you onstage at just the perfect time." And then she instructed me to give all my heart to the work God had put before me. At the end of the letter, she wrote Matthew 6:33: "But seek first his kingdom and his righteousness, and all these things will be given to you as well" (NIV).

That passage became my life verse; in many ways it is the banner God planted over my journey with him. When I don't know what to do, I always fall back into these words: "Seek first his kingdom."

I love to think things through, process the options, weigh the evidence, and come up with short directives that seem logical and sane. The reason and logic of this phrase always bring me back to center, to all that really matters: *Seek first his kingdom.* It makes sense to me. It realigns my priorities. It reminds me to focus on what I may have forgotten. And then there is the amazing promise attached to this instruction: *And all these things will be given to you as well.*

What things? All the things Jesus just talked to us about in verse 25. All the things you need to live. Whatever you will need for your body. Food. Clothes. Everything you will need for life, everything you and I might worry about, he promises to those who seek him first.

The journey of following Jesus with our lives involves two dimensions: everything we can do plus his divinity. This verse comes with challenge and instruction: Focus your heart. Ask God what's next. Rearrange your priorities. Actively work with your hands or your mind for his glory. And then, at the end of everything you can do, expect God's divine provision for "all these things."

For twenty years, I have kept track of my financial budget on a yellow pad. On the left-hand side, I make a list of the monthly bills, and on the right-hand side there is a column for every month. One of my greatest joys in life is writing "PAID" in the square that corresponds to the bills for that month. This last year I sat down to draw a new budget page on my yellow pad. At the top of the paper I wrote: "Watch God provide, again!" I have to tell you that when I wrote those words, I didn't know how he was going to do it. I saw all those little squares and it felt overwhelming to me. This month is October and I paid my bills yesterday. I sat at the kitchen table with tears in my eyes, looking at every square that had been marked paid for this year. I am so very grateful.

You know, this journey is a tough one. But I choose to believe that I am the little girl in the grown-up woman's body who is not making this journey alone. It is only when my heart is downcast and I have turned my eyes away from the kingdom that I believe I am by myself. I have heard the strong voice of Jesus reminding me to seek him first. More and more I am remembering who I belong to. Less and less I am listening to the fears of others.

I am going forward even when I cannot see. My worries are becoming trampled underneath the feet of my obedience. I sense the pleasure God takes in this offering.

Maybe the road is washed out ahead. Maybe others have turned around and given up. But I belong to Jesus and I will confidently expect a bridge.

From Longing to Hope

Paula Rinehart (*Better Than My Dreams*)

In this dilemma of living somewhere between entitlement and resignation—of letting our hearts go on a real journey with God—there are two women in Scripture whose stories continually intrigue me.

Hannah is a favorite of any woman who has longed to be a mother. You can see her pleading with God for a child, her heart so engaged she seems to be drunk. But she is not drinking; rather, she insists, her prayer is about her passionate longing for a child. She says, "I have poured out my soul before the LORD" (1 Sam. 1:15 NASB).

God gives her a son, Samuel, and with him the words that many a woman has claimed for the child of her prayers: "For this boy I prayed, and the LORD has given me my petition . . . So I have also dedicated him to the LORD; as long as he lives he is dedicated to the LORD" (1 Sam. 1:27–28 NASB).

Now notice how her story picks up in intensity. When Samuel is at the tender age of three, Hannah brings him back to the house of the Lord, where Eli will teach him what it means to serve God as a priest. Only Eli has failed miserably with his own sons, who are "worthless men," a disgrace to the priesthood (1 Sam. 2:12). Can you imagine how she felt leaving her small son to be cared for by this old man?

And what of Hannah's own dreams of being a mother and raising children? Hannah came once a year and brought Samuel a robe she'd made him, but she had no reason to think she would ever have another child.

What moves me about Hannah is the way she engaged God. Hers is that rare mixture of relentless hope and a surrendered heart. She asked God for the desire of her heart. And God asked her to do a very difficult thing with the gift of a son he gave.

I can never read the rest of her story without something melting inside me.

For as the saying goes, you can't outgive God. In the quaint words of the passage, "the LORD visited Hannah," and she gave birth to three sons and two daughters (1 Sam. 2:21 NASB). Her son Samuel, who grew up in the care of an old priest, became the greatest judge in Israel's history.

I return to Hannah's story whenever I need to be reminded that God honors our willingness to hope. When we bring our desires and longings to Jesus, he does something remarkable with them. It may not look like what we had in mind—but we do not hope in vain. I think of Hannah when I have forgotten to remember that often real hardship is the front edge of God's blessing.

The other woman at whose feet I sit is Naomi. When we meet her in Scripture, she is no spring chicken. She's old and worn out, defeated by famine and the loss of her husband and two sons. She is tired of living in a strange place. She has one more move left in her—her feet are set on returning to Israel.

Ruth, her Moabite daughter-in-law, insists on returning with Naomi, wanting to start life over together. But Naomi, like all of us at some points, cannot see past her losses. Just call me "Mara," she says, which is a name that means "bitter." She is resigned to a bleak future. "The hand of the Lord has gone forth against me," she says (Ruth 1:13 NASB). That's how she sees her life. *Just get me home, and I'll ask for nothing more.*

Have you ever allowed a rough time in your life to tilt your whole perspective? Do you find yourself reading your circumstances like tea leaves—and then misinterpreting your life? That was Naomi's story, and that's why the rest of the story is so encouraging.

God has more in mind for Naomi than she knows. For Ruth is going to marry Boaz. Ruth, the human embodiment of all Naomi has lost, is the woman through whom God will give Naomi something she would never have dreamed of. A son is born—Naomi's grandson—the gift of her old age, a child who rocks in her lap and nestles in her wrinkled arms.

As the light fades on the stage of Naomi's life, that's exactly where we are left—watching this defeated woman smile again. God does not leave her in some hopeless place she was only too willing to accept. For the story behind the story is this: the child she cradles is the grandfather of David, the father of the father of the father . . . of Jesus Christ. Naomi is a woman in Scripture whose life says, "Hold on, there's a bigger story." *There's a bigger story.*

So I ask God to keep my soul closer to that of Hannah's. I would rather live with a heart that is repeatedly poured out before the Lord, even if it's painful. And when I fall into Naomi's snare of just settling because I cannot believe God would meet me in this difficulty, then I pray my eyes will be opened to see what he might put in my own lap—because he is that good.

The thing I most want to hold on to in this journey with Christ is the wonder. *Oh, Lord,* I find myself praying, *let me look past the smoke from the ashes of my dreams and expectations until I find you.*

For Christ is—as the parable claims—the treasure hidden in a field, worth selling all we own to possess. And living your real life *with him* is, truly, where wonderful begins.

Part II

The Things
That Set Us Free

*"And let us run with perseverance
the race marked out for us."*

(Heb 12:1 NIV)

Embracing Prayer

God Is Listening

Sheila Walsh (*Get Off Your Knees and Pray*)

If you had asked me to describe my spiritual life when I was twenty years old, it would have sounded something like this: I love to read the Bible. I love reading spiritual classics. I am very involved in my church. And I am challenged in my prayer life.

At thirty, I would have said pretty much the same thing, except in regard to prayer I might have reduced "I am challenged" to "I stink." (I was beginning to be more honest about my life in my thirties.) But otherwise the facts would remain intact.

At forty, I would have added that I love talking to women about faith and fear, honesty and heartache. And I had pretty much resigned myself to "stinking" in my prayer life.

And now? Well, now I am fifty, and change in every arena of life has become an ongoing reality.

But I am discovering profound and simple gifts that have come with the passing years. I am changing in my understanding of my spiritual life. I am more inclined to listen for God's voice than to present to him a list of requests. I have a quiet confidence that no matter what seems to be true, God is always in control.

Most important, I have realized that it is not possible to stink at prayer. It might feel that way to us at times, but I believe that from God's perspective, he gladly receives our words and he sees our hearts. Any prayer is a gift to him, for it means we are talking to him. We just have to take that first step—and begin embracing prayer as part of our daily lives, as vital to us as breathing.

I no longer divide my life into the spiritual part and everything else. I believe when we recognize that God is always with us, every breath can be a prayer. Prayer is not just a few sentences we say to God while on our knees, but it is living out our ongoing, every-moment commitment to God.

Perhaps you're thinking, *Prayer is easy—we were made to rejoice in our relationship with God and to thank him for his gifts.* Well, sure, it's always easy to be thankful for God's good gifts. But what about when we're not thankful? What about when we're hurt? Angry? Numb? Is it so easy then?

It might not be so easy, but God wants it to be our first response.

Or perhaps you're thinking, *Prayer has never been easy for me. I do stink at it!* You feel like what you say to him is insincere, unsure. Or you question whether he even really cares to hear from you. Or you're so overwhelmed you don't even want to talk to him.

It isn't. He does. He still wants you to.

God hears all our prayers, the good and the bad. He is big enough to handle our honest questions and our doubts and even our anger. I sat beside a friend after she buried her child and listened as she poured out her raw emotions to God. Her prayer wasn't pretty, but it was from her heart and God knew it. I watched my son struggle with prayer after the death of his beloved grandfather: "Didn't you tell me, Mommy, that if I prayed God would answer? Well, I asked him not to take my papa and he did. Prayer doesn't work!" It hurt me immeasurably to see his pain, but I knew God was there with him. And I've blasted God with my own prayer challenges . . . and mumbled to him my doubts. And I know he heard me. He has heard you too.

God receives our prayers—the thankful ones and the not-so-thankful ones, the eloquent ones and the less-than-perfect ones. He accepts not only our joyful prayers and self-confident prayers but also the prayers we offer when we're not certain of things—or when we're not sure we really want the answer. He accepts our anguished questioning when we experience trauma or loss. He even accepts the prayers that beg him to rain down disaster on someone who has wounded us (although he may not answer them). He accepts all our prayers because they acknowledge we believe God is in control. When we're happy, when we're angry, when we're hurting to the point that words are lost and all we can offer is a cry for help—he is still there.

God is listening.

The bottom line is, life is hard. God knows all about it. And more than that, right in the center of the tornado of our lives, God offers a quiet place, a shelter where he waits with open arms and an open heart to embrace any of us who will come. Whether you are young or old, full of hope or full of fear, angry or excited, bitter or grateful, this remains my conviction: God is listening.

The Words We Pray

Marilyn Meberg (*Assurance of a Lifetime*)

Prayer is the key to accessing the power of the Holy Spirit within you. You open your mouth and use your words. You open your heart and reveal your concern. You unite with the Spirit in the knowledge he will answer you. In its most simplified form, that is prayer. Prayer is talking to God.

My daughter, Beth, is teaching her six-year-old son, Alec, to pray out loud. He has been reluctant to hear his own little voice addressing God. He's afraid his words "won't sound right." So Beth is coaching him on his words. When they come together to pray, Beth tells Alec she will say a phrase and then Alec can repeat the phrase. Beth will say another phrase, and Alec will repeat it.

Yesterday, before the evening meal, Alec was going to pray, again with his mother's coaching. The prayer began with, "Thank you, God, for this great day. Thank you for this food. And could you help me understand numbers?"

Alec's head shot up as Beth asked God for numerical assistance, and he said, "Can I say *that* to God?" He was astounded that prayer was not just thanking God for food and safety. It's also about the stuff in our lives and the needs of our souls. Understanding numbers is a basic need in Alec's life right now.

The moment we begin talking to God and making our needs known, we are accessing the power of the Spirit. The psalmist wrote that when we pray, God answers us. God hears us and begins immediately to help us with the concerns in our lives. First John 5:14–15 says: "We can be confident that he will listen to us whenever we ask him for anything in line with his will. And if we know he is listening when we make our requests, we can be sure that he will give us what we ask for" (NLT). That's why we talk to God about everything. He listens, he cares, and he works for us. That praying accesses the Spirit power within us.

Now, let's pause just a moment to key into a phrase in the 1 John verse. Notice that it says, "whenever we ask him for anything in line with his will." That phrase is a safety net for us. We may not always pray for what is within the will of God. For example, it is never in the will of God that we pray for something contrary to what is morally right. God has provided right-living standards for us, and it is never his will that we break those standards.

I love the way *The Message* translation of the Bible presents 1 Peter 1:17. It states: "You call out to God for help and he helps— he's a good Father that way. But don't forget, he's also a responsible Father, and won't let you get by with sloppy living."

There's great security in realizing we can pray for the desires of our heart while knowing God is not going to allow "sloppy living." We have the assurance of the Holy Spirit living within us. We have the assurance that prayer ignites his power to meet our needs. And we have the assurance that even when our prayer requests may be out of line, he will not let us get by with "sloppy living."

Prayer is talking to God. With confidence, we echo the wishes of David stated in Psalm 5:3: "Listen to my voice in the morning, LORD. Each morning I bring my requests to you and wait expectantly" (NLT).

What Does the Bible Tell Us About Prayer?
Sheila Walsh (*Get Off Your Knees and Pray*)

As I pored over the Scriptures, searching for what God has to say about prayer, several things became immediately clear:

- We are called to pray with a clean heart: "If I regard iniquity in my heart, the Lord will not hear. But certainly God has heard me; He has attended to the voice of my prayer" (Ps. 66:18–19 NKJV).

- We are called to pray, believing: "And whatever things you ask in prayer, believing, you will receive" (Matt. 21:22 NKJV).
- We are called to pray in Christ's name: "And whatever you ask in My name, that I will do, that the Father may be glorified in the Son" (John 14:13 NKJV).
- We are called to pray according to the Father's will: "Now this is the confidence that we have in Him, that if we ask anything according to His will, He hears us" (1 John 5:14 NKJV).

On second thought, even with these "clear" instructions, I still had questions. So I took a closer look at these four directives.

A CLEAN HEART

According to Psalm 66:18, our purity of heart is so essential that if we "regard iniquity in [our] heart, the Lord will not hear" (NKJV). And in Psalm 51:10, David urges God to give him "a clean heart" (NKJV).

What exactly is a "clean heart"? How clean, exactly? Scrubbed-spotless-till-you-can-see-your-reflection clean? Or quick-tidy-up-before-the-guests-arrive clean?

As women, our hormones lead us on a lively dance for most of our lives. So what do we do on those "days of the month" when we don't feel very holy or sometimes even sane? Does God hear our prayers when our emotions are taking us on a roller coaster ride? What if we want to have a clean heart, but we're having trouble with it? What if we believe we have a clean heart, but there is some little seed of unforgiveness buried deep inside us we've forgotten all about? Are we responsible only for the sins we remember or for every little offense we've committed over our entire lifetime?

I received a letter from a woman who had been sexually abused by her father when she was a child. Her concern was that there were months of this devastating time in her childhood she had blocked out. She simply couldn't remember what had happened. "How can I come to God with a clean heart when I can't remember so much of that horrible time? Will God hold that against me?" she asked.

My heart ached for this woman who had already suffered so much and was now tormented by the thought that the offenses acted out upon her would hinder her prayers and follow her for the rest of her life. I wanted to tell her that part of the miracle of prayer is that God knows what we need before we even ask him. When it is our earnest desire to be clean, God sees that—whether we can remember every detail of our lives or not. Yes, God wants us to come before him with a pure heart, but he also tells us that he hears our honest petitions. Notice what verse 19 of Psalm 66 says: "Certainly God has heard me."

We can't keep worrying about how clean the corners of our soul are. If we get caught up in that whirlpool of self-loathing and doubt, we're only headed down. But if we come before the God who makes all things new, believing in faith that he knows our true hearts, we are certain to be uplifted.

BELIEVING

Surely Jesus' words recorded in Matthew 21:22 have caused much confusion among believers: "And whatever things you ask in prayer, believing, you will receive." "Whatever" covers a lot of ground.

Perhaps you have been exposed to prosperity teaching, which seems to advocate "if you can name it, you can claim it; if you can mark it, you can park it!" This theology is not an accurate understanding of what the Bible teaches. Prosperity teaching takes the wonderful truth that our Father is the King of kings and reduces it to the conclusion that we should all then live like royalty on this earth.

For instance, I was channel surfing one night and landed on a religious talk show. Three college students were being interviewed about their faith. One girl held up a picture of a red Mercedes convertible and announced proudly that this was what she was "believing" for. As though that's what Jesus had in mind for her!

But beyond the self-indulgent misinterpretations of this verse is a much more serious heart cry from those who long for God to intervene when life is falling apart and who can't understand why he doesn't appear to hear their prayers. From 1987 to 1992, I was cohost of *The 700 Club* with Pat Robertson. I received hundreds of letters from viewers who stumbled over this misunderstanding of prayer. They said things like:

- "I prayed in faith that my husband would be healed of cancer, but he died. What did I do wrong?"

- "I have given and given to the church and this ministry believing for a miracle in my own finances, but I am still in debt. What am I doing wrong?"
- "I have kept myself pure and prayed, believing that God would bring me a husband, and I am still alone. Why isn't God honoring my prayers?"

I witnessed such torment in people's lives. Many felt they were doing something wrong, and if they could just find out what the key was, things would been different. Can you imagine the agony of believing your child or your husband would not have died if you had somehow worked out this puzzle in time? Or the pain of the woman who sits home alone wondering where her soul mate is as she watches the years pass by, taking with them her ability to be a mother?

To these situations, add the agony of silence. If you believe that somehow whatever reality you are living in is your fault, who do you dare talk to? How can you voice these things aloud and risk seeing disapproval in the eyes of someone else?

I think this verse has left many sitting alone and lost. I'll be honest: there's no easy answer. But I think part of the problem is that we tend to focus on only one part of that scripture. We want to hear all about the "receiving" side of things—*What are you going to do for me, God? Why haven't you given me what I asked for?*—rather than the "believing" side—*God, I believe in you 100 percent and know you love me, and today that's all that matters.* God has and always will have our best interests at heart. Just as our children look at us in faith, knowing we love them and will take care of them, we need to do the same with our heavenly Father. I'm not saying that will always be easy; we might want to stomp our foot or cry into our pillows. But we have to trust that God will make all things clear some day.

IN JESUS' NAME

In John's Gospel we read that whatever prayers we ask in Jesus' name will be answered so that God the Father will be glorified (14:13). This is such an incredible gift. But . . . the authority we're given can be a dangerous thing. I think it's easy to tag "In Jesus' name, amen" to the end of our prayers without thinking through the full implications of what that means.

Coming in someone's name means you represent that person—you have been granted the authority to speak for that person. For example, when police officers or FBI agents present themselves at someone's home, they produce identification to show that they have the authority of the agency they represent behind them. Likewise, when we say, "In Jesus' name," we are saying we are on royal business. Understanding that has helped me be bold in prayer but also be careful that my requests are in keeping with the character of Christ. I have a fresh sense of what an honor it is to be able to come to God in his Son's name, and I work hard not to abuse the privilege.

ACCORDING TO THE FATHER'S WILL

In John's first letter, he clarifies that we are to ask according to the Father's will, and he will hear us (5:14). What exactly does that mean? How do we keep from replacing his wishes with our own? Even more, how do we even know what the Father's will is in any given situation? To my human understanding, it would always seem to be God's will to heal a child or a broken marriage. Wouldn't such a miracle bring glory to God? What about when a child prays a simple prayer of faith in Jesus' name? Surely God would answer that.

My son faced this heartbreaking dilemma when he was just four years old. My father-in-law, William Pfaehler, lived with us for two years after the death of his wife, Eleanor. Having him in our home was a wonderful gift to all of us, but especially to Christian. He loved his papa so much, and they had a lot of fun together. One night when my husband, Barry, was in Florida, William had a heart attack and collapsed in his bathroom. Christian and I sat with him until the paramedics arrived. He was still breathing when they loaded him into the ambulance, but his lips were very blue. Christian and I followed the ambulance to the hospital. When we arrived, the doctor informed us that William had not survived the trip.

Christian was quiet as we drove home. All he said that night was, "I'm going to miss my papa."

He grieved openly for weeks, and then one day I saw a flash of anger cross his face as he brushed our cat, Lily, off the sofa. I suggested that we take a walk, and I asked him if he was angry. With his customary honesty, he told me he was.

"You told me, Mom, that Jesus listens to our prayers and answers them. Well, I asked God not to take my papa, and he did anyway. So what's the point?"

I felt my son's pain. (Is there a believer alive who hasn't thought that same thing when it seemed as if heaven was silent to his or her cries?) At his tender age, my son had to experience what it means to pray according to the Father's will, whether or not he—or I—understood it.

There is obviously much more to this thing called prayer than what we currently know.

8

Studying the Bible

Liberated by Truth

Sheila Walsh (*I'm Not Wonder Woman*)

I enjoy studying. I love the process of digging deep into a subject that I know very little about and gleaning from the wisdom of those whose life's work has been to unpack its mysteries. I discovered when I went to graduate school in the fall of 1993, however, that there is a right way to study and a wrong way. Graduate school papers have to be presented in a certain layout, using either *The Chicago Manual of Style* or a similar style guide. I had no idea that such a thing existed, but had I heard the phrase dropped in conversation, I would have assumed it had to do with how to accessorize a suit.

My first class in seminary was in church history. I scanned the list of possible research topics as the professor explained the requirements of the paper. The paper had to be twenty-five pages long and had to include a bibliography of reference material with the appropriate footnotes and endnotes. He ended by telling us, "Fifty percent of your grade will be based on your research paper, which must be turned in two weeks before the end of the semester."

Fifty percent! For the next few nights, I sat at my desk at home and wrestled with the task of writing this paper. I didn't know what a footnote or an endnote was. A footnote sounded like a "P.S." and I thought an endnote might be the "Amen!" I had imagined that all I had to do was write the paper and have it typed up so that it was neat with no telltale signs of coffee spilled on the pages and no bits chewed by Abigail, my cat. I realized that I was in over my head. After the next class, I asked the professor if I could talk to him.

"I don't know how to do this," I admitted.

"What do you mean?" he asked kindly.

"Well, I've never written a paper for a graduate class, and I honestly don't know where to start."

For thirty minutes, the professor sat with me and went over each step: how to research, how to catalog the research, how the finished paper should look. He helped me to understand how to access knowledge, how to read a book so that I will understand it, grasp hold of what is being said, and then determine if I agree with the writer. I left that meeting grateful for his guidance and guidelines. I felt less ignorant, more confident that I could take one step at a time. I was also deeply grateful to God for setting me free from the fear of asking for help or admitting that I needed it.

I have discovered that study is a faithful friend if we learn its ways. I see that a great deal of damage is done, not by evil, but by ignorance. Christ tells us that we will know the truth and the truth will set us free (John 8:32), but so often we don't know what the truth is. We don't know how to dig it out.

In Romans, Paul tells us that our lives are to be transformed by the renewing of our minds. But if we have no firm grasp on what God's Word says, how can we be changed by it? You will know the truth, and the truth will set you free, but first, you have to know it!

There is nothing in life more important than understanding God's truth and being changed by it. God has given us a mind so that we can learn and grow. As his people, we have a great responsibility and wonderful privilege of growing in our understanding of him. When we dig deep, there are hidden treasures to be found.

> Your Word is like a flaming sword
> A sharp and mighty arrow
> A wedge that cleaves the rock;
> That word can pierce through heart and marrow
> Oh, send it forth o'er all the earth
> To purge unrighteous leaven
> And cleanse our hearts for heaven.[1]

Dusting Off Your Bible: Where to Start if You're a Bit Out of Practice

Marilyn Meberg (*Assurance of a Lifetime*)

When my son Jeff was five years old, I snuggled up with him one evening shortly before his bedtime and suggested we read a Bible story together. Always sensitive about hurting others' feelings, Jeff hesitated and then asked, "Is there anything else we could do?"

"Well, what do you have in mind?" I asked.

"How about chocolate chip ice cream? We could each have a bowl," he answered. So we both had a bowl of chocolate chip ice cream and *then* read a Bible story together.

Matthew 5:6 states, "Blessed are those who hunger and thirst for righteousness, for they shall be filled" (NKJV). One of the ways we are "filled" and satisfied is by studying the Bible.

So how does one start studying the Bible? First, you want to be aware that the Bible is not just a moral guidebook or a list of directions for better living. Though you will be inspired by its moral teachings and will certainly learn principles meant to save you from the consequences of poor decisions, the Bible is more than that. It is a divinely inspired Book meant to communicate a personal message: God knew you and loved you before he even made you. That message is expressed throughout the Bible in passages like this one: "Long before he laid down earth's foundations, he had us in mind, had settled on us as the focus of his love" (Eph. 1:4 MSG).

You will find this theme throughout the Bible. The Bible is

God's voice speaking that message of passionate love to each of us. He is exceedingly passionate about his creation!

So where do you begin? Because the Bible is literally a library of books, you can begin reading anywhere. Should you start at the very beginning and begin reading Genesis? You certainly can. But I would suggest you begin reading the first four books in the New Testament because there you get a great picture of who Jesus is, what he said, what he did, and why he did it. Those books—Matthew, Mark, Luke, and John—are similar because all four are accounts of Jesus' life. They are wonderfully instructive; as you read them, you will become increasingly familiar with Jesus. You will hear from him again and again the theme that we, God's creation, were, are, and will always be the "focus of his love."

Linger as long as you want in those books. By studying them, you are receiving foundational truth as you assimilate what you learn about Jesus, something that is very satisfying for you who "hunger and thirst." When you feel like it, I'd suggest you then begin reading the book of Acts.

Acts details what happened after Jesus left the earth. The disciples were told to get out there and spread the good news of Jesus. The book chronicles the beginning of the first Christian church and many of the harrowing experiences that contributed to its growth. Jesus told the disciples their jobs would not be greater than their abilities because the Holy Spirit would enable them when they felt weak and afraid. You will remember one of the great sports for the Romans in those days was feeding Christians to the lions. You can imagine the need, then, for the empowering of the Holy Spirit for those early Christians! Many died for their faith. (In these cases the Spirit did not empower them to rip open the jaws of the attacking lions.)

We also see in the book of Acts how Christianity rose out of Judaism. The early Christians acknowledged Jesus as the Messiah, but these new Christians remained deeply committed to their Jewish traditions. They struggled when the Holy Spirit nudged them to take the message of Jesus' love to the Gentiles. It did not make sense to them that God could possibly love the Gentiles and that Jesus' death on the cross offered forgiveness for Gentiles' sin as well as their own.

Also in Acts you will read about Paul, a highly educated and articulate Jewish scholar who despised all he heard about the impostor-Messiah named Jesus. Paul, with his intellect and political power, was determined to see that all Christians were tortured, imprisoned, or murdered for their offensive faith in Jesus. However, God had Paul in mind long before the foundations of the earth were laid. Paul was the "focus" of God's love. You'll be fascinated with the account of Paul's trip to Damascus. I'm sure you can guess what happened.

If I found myself exiled to the little town of Abscessed Molar, Texas (ten miles south of Puffy Gums), and was given a choice of what Bible book I could take with me, it would be the book of Romans. It follows the book of Acts.

After Paul's dramatic conversion, he responded to the

passionate love of God by teaching, preaching, and writing about the Jesus he came to know personally and love intensely. The book of Romans is a long letter Paul wrote to a group of first-century Christians in Rome. In it he brilliantly and passionately described how it is possible that sinful human beings can find acceptance with God. It is in Romans that we read, "There is no condemnation for those who belong to Christ Jesus" (8:1 NLT). Not only are we accepted by God but also our sin no longer condemns us. We are free from the sin shackles that enslaved us and kept us in bondage. What is the source of that freedom? Jesus! His death on the cross for all sin puts us in the elite category of those without condemnation.

Romans 5:1–2 says, "Since we have been made right in God's sight by faith, we have peace with God because of what Jesus Christ our Lord has done for us. Because of our faith, Christ has brought us into this place of highest privilege where we now stand, and we confidently and joyfully look forward to sharing God's glory" (NLT).

What peace and sweet assurance those words produce! Such words, inspired by the Holy Spirit of God within the born-again spirit of Paul, cause us to again see the depth of God's focused love for us. Romans is a book you will want to read over and over again. I wouldn't go into exile without it. In fact, I don't want to go anywhere without it.

Now, you may be wondering about the Old Testament and when you should start reading it. You can, of course, start anytime. My suggestion, however, is that after you've absorbed the life and words of Jesus, and after you read Acts and Romans, you then begin reading the Old Testament.

I recommend that you begin by reading the people stories. There are many people stories in Genesis, and there are also full books of people stories: Joshua, Ruth, Ezra, Job, Jonah, and Hosea, for example. I'd suggest you read the entire story of each person rather than stop at the end of a chapter within the book. (Someone else can cook dinner!) I love reading these stories because I see myself in so many of them. Though centuries, customs, and languages separate us, we are united by the same heart cries. And in all that we read, we are the focused love of God.

The book of Psalms is a compilation of prayers meant to be prayed aloud. You'll see that there is nothing polished or refined about the language in these prayers. They are sometimes whiny, happy, confused, faltering, repetitious, and uncertain. In other words, they use real words to express real emotion. You can literally pray the book of Psalms to God.

I suggest you save the prophetic books of Isaiah, Jeremiah, and Ezekiel until a later study. The same is true for the books of God's law: Leviticus, Numbers, and Deuteronomy. You will ultimately benefit from reading them, but it's okay to wait awhile before you dive into them.

And by the way, it's always beneficial to have a standard study Bible to help you in your understanding of Scripture. Study Bibles have notes and cross-references that help you understand each passage and put it into perspective.

Finally, I strongly urge you to get involved in a group Bible study. I'm a firm believer in the value each of us brings to the other. As you study together, share together, and pray together, a rich bond is established. That bond deepens as you feel loved and accepted by each other. Together you grow in your understanding of what it means to be a Christian and what it means to be the passionate focus of God's love.

Also, I'm sure that environment could be greatly enriched by the occasional sharing of chocolate chip ice cream.

Building Your Life on a Solid Rock, Verse by Verse

Angela Thomas (*When Wallflowers Dance; A Beautiful Offering*)

One thing I've learned is that you begin to believe what you focus on, whether it's actually true or not. I have personally focused on my rejection in various areas of career and relationships and then began to live as though I was worthy of only rejection. I have believed what I have focused on. That trash is a complete mind game formulated by Satan to steal our dreams and our confidence. That kind of mental garbage will take you down and keep you there. But it's all a lie.

These mistaken beliefs will limit and frustrate the work God intends to do. And nothing will happen in your life, I mean a big, fat nothing—until you begin to focus on the truth of God.

Jesus says to us in John 15:7 (NIV): If you remain in me and my words remain in you, ask whatever you wish, and it will be given you.

I realize that you probably already have heard about and believe in the importance of reading the Bible. It's just that very few of us have made a commitment to stay in the words of God, no matter what. Even when your heart is dry. Even when you feel no emotion or seem to get nowhere when reading a passage. Stay in there and keep these anointed words "abiding" in your mind and heart. Remember these reasons to study the Bible from the book of Psalms:

> The teachings of the LORD are perfect; they give new
> strength.
> The rules of the LORD can be trusted; they make plain
> people wise.
> *The orders of the LORD are right; they make people happy.*
> *The commands of the LORD are pure; they light up the way.*
> (19:7–8 NCV, emphasis mine)

Plan how you are going to read the Bible so that you don't get it in your hand and have no idea where to turn. Keep a Bible in every room of your house and in the car so that it's always within reach. Read different versions of Scripture to hear a fresh understanding of a passage you've heard only a certain way. Memorize the books of the Bible in order so that it's easy to get around and you feel comfortable finding your way.

As you make this commitment to consistently read the Bible, everything in the world will happen to distract you from keeping it. Realize what's happening: a spiritual battle. Stay in there. Fight to get to the Word. God has promised that his words will never return void. That means his words will always be powerful, especially when they have been taken deep into your life. Daily, no matter what, keep reading and meditating on God's words to you.

How do you eat an elephant? One little bite at a time. Beginning to put on the words of Jesus may feel like an elephant to you. It can to me. Sometimes I am overwhelmed by all the change that needs to happen in my life. Sometimes I am fatigued by the endlessness of the journey. Sometimes I think that I just can't become amazing because I'm not strong enough or brave enough.

Because of my schedule and the schedules of the children, I live by one cardinal rule . . . do what's next. I will have a melt-down if I try to work on a project that's two weeks out. All I can do is what's required next. The width of my reach may broaden when the children are older, but for now, I have calendars every-where, field trip schedules posted, and my schedule outlined beside theirs with spelling tests and book deadlines thrown in for extra stress. All I can do is take the next step. Pack the next lunch. Fold another load of clothes. Do the next thing, however small it may seem.

I want to have a great big understanding of Jesus and God's Word. I want to know the Bible and take it into my life. But some days I have to approach my spiritual life like it's an elephant. I give myself grace when all I can do is take the small bite. Do the next thing. Read one chapter that I ponder through the day. Write a few words in my journal that give insight to my heart. Respond to an injustice more like Jesus and less like me. Try to be faithful, even in small ways, even though I wish I could tackle it all at once.

Jesus said that we are supposed to build our house on the rock. The rock that he is referring to is himself. We are supposed to build our lives on the solid foundation of Jesus. Maybe you have already begun. Maybe you have been delayed. Maybe it seems like an elephant that you can't tackle. But is there one small step you can take? One small bite that will get you started?

In our relationship with Jesus, all he requires is that we do the next thing. The next thing for you may mean getting yourself back into his presence and then learning to stay there consistently. It may mean praying about a specific weakness and then responding when God gives direction. It might mean stepping into an unknown or taking a risk or stretching yourself in ways you had not anticipated. However small the step, it is a step in the direction of Jesus and his likeness.

The amazing life, the beautiful offering, the life God dreamed of for you and me begins on the solid foundation of Jesus Christ. I imagine some of you have already known the sinking sand of many other beginnings. It's okay. Tear it all down and start over right. Come back to the only sure footing. We get to start over with God. We get second chances and new beginnings and renewed dreams. It is never too late to build an amazing life with Christ.

The Bible Is on My Side

Stormie Omartian (*Finding Peace for Your Heart*)

I had given up trying to read the Bible years ago when several unsuccessful attempts brought discouragement and frustration. I found the writing so foreign I couldn't understand it at all. But our pastor taught from the Scriptures with amazing clarity, and I hung on every word. It was like watching a movie so reflective of my own life that I became involved in the action.

Could it be, I asked myself, *that I might feel that same way when I read the Bible at home alone?*

The next morning I began reading in Psalms and Proverbs, which had short chapters and seemed to be safe enough for me to tackle. Over the following weeks I branched out in the Gospels of Matthew, Mark, Luke, and John. I was surprised at the way every word came alive with new meaning. Soon I had such a desire to know the whole story that I started at the beginning of the Bible and read straight through to the end. When I finished months later, I felt as if I knew the heart of the Author and my life had been changed.

While I was reading semi-faithfully each day, I noticed distinct and undeniable benefits. For example, I had been experiencing difficulty in thinking clearly, yet I found that I had noticeable mental clarity after I read the Bible. I discovered it was especially beneficial to read Scripture the first thing in the morning because it set my heart and mind on the right course for the day. Also reading the Bible before I went to bed at night ensured that I would sleep without nightmares, which had been a problem for as long as I could remember.

Gradually the Bible became God's voice in my ear. When I heard certain old, familiar words in my mind, such as *You're worthless. You'll never amount to anything. Why try?* I also heard the words of God saying, *You are fearfully and wonderfully made. I will lift you up from the gates of death. You will be blessed if you put your trust in me* (Ps. 139:14; 9:13; 2:12).

The more I read, the more I saw that God's laws were good. They were there for my benefit, and I could trust them. It became clear to me that conscience wasn't an adequate indicator of right or wrong. I could see that things can really only be found right or wrong in the light of God's Word. Such guidelines, rather than restricting, were actually liberating to me.

You may be thinking, *I can't afford the time it takes to read the Bible every day.* Reading God's Word must become a daily discipline because we need a solid grasp of the way God intends us to live. The Bible says, "Man shall not live by bread alone, but by every word that proceeds from the mouth of God" (Matt. 4:4 NKJV). Regular feeding on God's Word satisfies the hunger of our souls and keeps us from emotional depletion and spiritual starvation.

At times in my battle with fear and depression I sat down to read the Word of God feeling so depleted, numb, or preoccupied with my mental state that I could hardly even comprehend the words. I not only didn't feel close to God but also felt it futile to hope he could ever change me or my life in any lasting way. In spite of that, as I read I was struck by a remarkable lifting of those negative emotions. Afterward I may not have been able to pass a Bible school quiz on the passage, but I left renewed, strengthened, and hopeful.

When you feel confused, fearful, depressed, or anxious, take the Bible in hand and say, "This book is on my side. My soul is starving, and this is food for my spirit. I want to do the right thing and reading the Bible is always the right thing to do. Lord, I thank you for your Word. Reveal yourself to me as I read it and let it come alive in my heart and mind. Show me what I need to know for my life today. Let your Word penetrate through anything that would block me from receiving it." Then begin to read until you sense peace coming into your heart.

While the Bible was written to give you knowledge of the Lord, it takes the Holy Spirit to bring a particular Scripture alive to your heart. When that happens, take it as God speaking words of comfort, hope, and guidance directly to you. The Bible says, "For whatever things were written before were written for our learning, that we through the patience and comfort of the Scriptures might have hope" (Rom. 15:4 NKJV).

Don't say, "I've already read the Bible, I've memorized a hundred Scriptures, and I even teach Bible classes, so I don't need to read it every day." This is dangerous thinking. Whenever you eat food or drink water, you don't say, "I won't have to do that again," do you? Of course not. Your body needs to be fed daily. The same goes for your spiritual and emotional self. And because you're not the same person today as you were the day before, you will receive from God's Word in a new and different way today. In fact, if you've read your Bible many, many times, buy a *new* Bible in a different translation or the same translation in a different form, and read it through again. You'll be surprised how new and fresh the Word is to you.

It helps to keep in mind that the Bible is God's love letter to *you*. When you receive letters from someone you love, you don't just read them once and never look at them again. You pore over them time after time, drinking in the very essence of that person, looking between the lines for any and every possible message. God's love letters to you are full of messages. They say, "This is how much I love you." They do *not* say, "These are the things you need to do to *get* me to love you." The Bible is not just a collection of information; it is a book of life. It's not to be read as a ritual or out of fear that something bad will happen if you don't. It's to be read so God can build you up in his love from the inside out and brand his nature into your heart so that nothing can keep you away from his presence.

9

Learning to Be Authentic

The Big Cover-Up

Lisa Whittle (*Behind Those Eyes*)

In 1994, I was a graduate student in Texas, struggling to pay my rent on a shoestring salary. Already working two jobs to make ends meet, I determined that I needed another supplemental income. My friend Martie asked me about my interest in working in the cosmetics industry, and I jumped at the idea. I had always looked at the salespeople behind the cosmetics counters and wished I were as beautiful and put together as they appeared to be. And besides that, I loved to experiment with makeup.

After being hired by a well-established company and undergoing some training, I was on my way. It didn't take me long to learn the tricks of the trade, the artistry of applying makeup, and how to close a sale. I thoroughly enjoyed my job and always looked forward to my time at the counter.

I saw many different types of customers while working in cosmetics; a Saturday shift at the mall was a fascinating experiment in people watching. I have since forgotten many of the faces I saw while working at the makeup counter in Texas. But one customer, I can assure you, I will never, ever forget.

She approached the counter like many others, rather timid and lacking confidence, as I had seen in other women before. But she was noticeably different, right from the start. Wearing a hat pulled down on her forehead and thick, dark sunglasses, she paused for a minute and then finally spoke. "Good morning," she said. "Can you help me?" She removed her glasses, and although she was a grown woman, the look in her eyes was that of a schoolgirl waiting for her punishment from a stern principal.

I paused before I answered, taking in the sight before me. I was glad she couldn't read my thoughts. *Whoa. Those are some pretty bad scars. I hope she doesn't want me to try to cover them up. Yikes! Do we even make a product that will cover up burns? What happened to her? I feel so sorry for her.* I wasn't altogether sure I could help her, but I welcomed her to the counter anyway. "Well, ma'am, I'm not sure, but let's give it a shot!" The woman looked genuinely relieved that we had gotten past the introduction and clearly now felt a bit safer with me.

"I need something to cover these up," she continued, pointing to the scars I had already noticed. I took a deep breath, said a silent prayer, and began to try to recall my training in makeup application, though I am convinced that all the training in the world would not have been particularly helpful at the moment.

The badly scarred woman and I worked together to see what result we could get with what we had. For the next thirty minutes, we experimented with colors and textures and consistencies of makeup. With me determined to help her and her willing to let me, we dabbled in different application techniques and tricks of concealment. It took nearly an hour total before we were satisfied with the result even though it was not a perfect solution to her problem. She left that day feeling a little better about what she saw when she looked in the mirror. But what our meeting triggered in me has lasted many years.

No, these women weren't coming to me for counseling, but many of them came to the counter looking to change something they didn't like about themselves. They sought this change with makeup and cosmetics on the outside. But all of them were trying to conceal things about themselves in order to hide the truth and escape rejection from others.

This story brings me to an important question to consider in this great charade in life we play. How many of us are trying to conceal our feelings to cover up our broken souls? We do this so others will see on the outside what we want them to see. We think we can fool people with our cover-ups, and maybe we can. But God wants us to be *real* . . . real to others, real to ourselves, and real with him. Whether we are feeling insecure, jealous, lonely, or afraid, our precious Father desires to hold us and tell us we are worthy, important, gifted, and never alone. We are never to fear. He longs to uncover these feelings we hide so that we can find out who we are, once and for all . . . without all the concealer.

Hiding from God, Hiding from Each Other
Jill Hubbard (*The Secrets Women Keep*)

I believe the secrets we women are keeping are slowly but surely destroying us. That's a pretty dramatic statement, I know. But think about it. A secret eats away at you, and as time passes, it seems to grow and fester. It becomes more and more of a burden.

When we are going through life acting as one person on the outside, while we're really a different person on the inside, we can't have peace. We know something's off. There's an acute sense of dissonance when our interiors and exteriors don't match. It's as if we are an orchestra and the brass is playing a Mozart concerto while the strings are playing a Beethoven sonata. It sounds awful! We cringe at the dreadful sounds—and when we have secrets, our hearts and souls cringe at the terrible noise within us.

It requires an enormous reservoir of energy to maintain two distinct selves—the external front we show the world and the internal, *true* self. This pretense drains us and robs us of the energy we could be using in countless other ways, from improving our relationships to deepening our spiritual lives to putting the laundry away and making dinner. The more aligned we are, internally and externally, the more real we can be. We simply can't live full, passionate lives of integrity if we are not being authentic. Having secrets is a sure way to avoid authenticity.

The truth is, as much as we might feel safe in hiding our secrets, we know we can't hide from God. So we are really just fooling ourselves. "'Can anyone hide in secret places so that I cannot see him?' declares the LORD. 'Do not I fill heaven and earth?'" (Jer. 23:24 NIV). Realizing we can't hide from God makes us feel a bit foolish when we're using all our resources to stay hidden. But still, we rationalize that even though God can see us, it's okay to keep things hidden from other people.

The Bible repeatedly calls us out of the darkness and into the light. Jesus warns that it's futile to try to keep things hidden. He said, "There is nothing concealed that will not be disclosed, or hidden that will not be made known" (Matt. 10:26 NIV).

When we keep secrets about ourselves, it's like we're constantly saying, "I'm not good enough. The truth about me is *not okay*." And when we have something to hide, it affects how we approach every aspect of life. It holds us back from engaging in true intimacy. It keeps us from living fully and expressing ourselves honestly. And it makes us unable to fully accept the love, grace, and forgiveness that God is eager to give.

As women we tend to assume that we're alone in our problems. We often think that nobody else feels this or feels that as strongly and deeply as we do while all along thousands of others are suffering alone, thinking nobody else could possibly understand. We don't know what's going on with other women. We only know what they allow us to see—what they present as their public persona. So what we end up doing is comparing our *insides* to other women's *outsides*. We believe that other women's external appearance represents all of who they really are—when that's not the case. Our exterior, public selves are only part of who we are. Women often have an active and rich internal world with a rapid running commentary. The critical committee, the doubting dialogue, and our shameful or sinful secrets all keep us fearing we'll be the only one who doesn't have it all together; therefore, our secrets stay just that.

It's a vicious cycle. We keep our failures and weaknesses to ourselves so others don't see the real us. They, in turn, don't feel they can reveal their own secrets because it appears that everyone around them is basically perfect. We are all busy perfecting our facades, suffering alone, assuming we're the *only ones* with this particular problem. And all the while we're surrounded by others suffering alone in their own pain.

Owning Our Stuff

Paula Rinehart (*Better Than My Dreams*)

Chris was a capable woman who led the children's program in a large church. What no one knew, though, was that Chris was also addicted to prescription pain medication. A severe neck injury and the stress of her life combined to grease the skids for a slow slide into drug dependence. By the time I met her, she was spending huge sums of money ordering painkillers off the Internet without her doctor's knowledge. Living in the hazy world of addiction, Chris was very much alone.

"Perhaps now is the time to step down from your position, tell your pastoral staff, and get some help for this," I suggested gently. "People rarely get past a drug dependence alone. It's a real battle."

Just the thought that others would know her struggle was more than Chris could bear. She could beat this if she tried hard, surely she could. Her order this month was less than the month before—she was making progress. And then she added a comment that stopped me short.

"Besides, I'm living under grace," she said. "And grace means that I'm forgiven, so I don't have to tell."

I took a deep breath. "No," I replied. "Grace means that because you are loved, you can come clean."

Coming clean. Being forgiven. Owning your stuff. How do we account for the miracle, really, of this great, wide mercy in Christ that allows us to name the worst about ourselves—and still be loved? What do we make of a grace that insists the truth can be told when it needs to be? For the very mercy that gives us a place in the Father's love even when our soul is in shambles holds something more: we get the chance to exhale in the presence of others. You can stop trying so hard to keep up the appearance of this woman who has all her flaws tucked in (which, of course, they never are).

The possibility of being human—being real with others—comes into view. You get to be at home in your own skin, able to offer a relationship to others that is more than just peeking out from behind a mask. Oh, what a relief.

I am convinced that being on a journey with the Lord down this rather narrow path leads to an incredibly spacious place. The ability to own your stuff with God and with others is the wildest freedom on the planet. And it is possible in Christ in ways that psychology and self-help and wishful thinking cannot begin to touch.

Getting Honest with God

Paula Rinehart (*Better Than My Dreams*)

What I hope you hear in this, at the roots of your being, is the preposterous willingness of God to meet you wherever you are . . . and to bring you home. Maybe you haven't opened a Bible in fifteen years. Perhaps you've thought of leaving your husband and no one knows. Or maybe your love for God has become so dishrag dull you understand full well how attractive a new shade of psychology could be. When you hear the phrase *owning your stuff*, what actually comes to mind?

We get honest with God (or anyone, really) as we come to hope that what awaits is not his judgment but his kindness. The love of God always comes with a bit of surprise. We've never been loved like that, not even close. There is no one in the universe who knows us to such depths—and yet embraces us in a love as vast as the mercy that flows from the cross of Christ.

Yet few of us live in the light of that acceptance. Brennan Manning, who writes about intimacy with God, once noted that the obstacles to experiencing that seem different for men and women. Men, he claims, are more often held back by their own pride. But women? What keeps us distant and aloof and believing we have to handle things ourselves? After years of offering spiritual direction to many folks, Brennan believes that women fall prey to internal barriers such as self-condemnation.[1]

In our hearts we believe that God is just like us—that is, he's waiting to read off a litany of complaints and reprimands. "You thought I was altogether like you," God says (Ps. 50:21 NIV). Meaning, of course, that since I would mark my name off the list of favored children, God would all the more.

"Therefore there is now no condemnation for those who are in Christ Jesus," the apostle Paul writes in Romans 8:1 (NIV). How often have you heard that verse—at a funeral or in a sermon, per-haps? Have you ever really heard those words in your personal life, though—in the sealed-off places in your own heart that no one can see?

As the old expression goes, "There are parts of me that have never heard the gospel." This is so true. If I let the love and for-giveness of God into those corners of my soul, no condemnation means that I see God waiting for me—not with a scowl on his face but with arms that embrace a daughter who knows she is home.

Listen to the refreshing, intimate way one man describes such a moment with God when he realized his own sin. He writes:

> I am overwhelmed by the utterly spare truthfulness of these things, as God has shown them to me without rancor, *without condemnation*. And I feel strangely relieved, cleansed, and unburdened. To have seen these things with Him, and not in opposition to Him—I see them simply falling away, out of my life (emphasis added).[2]

That God would love us in our shame—that he would offer to lead you into the essence of what you may be searching for in many futile places . . . who ever expects to be loved like this? His kindness is, truly, a wonder—and it is the very thing that makes it possible for our lives to change.

Getting Honest with Each Other
Paula Rinehart (*Better Than My Dreams*)

When I'm struggling to lay hold of honesty and humility in a relationship, I sometimes have flashbacks of my son at two years old, in that stage of orneriness that makes you want to hire a nanny. Caught in some flagrant act of willfulness, Brady would reap his just recompense. I'd put him on my lap and comfort him through his tears, trying to instill the art of confession.

"Now, Brady, you need to say you're sorry," I'd tell him, hoping to prompt an ounce or two of contrition.

Without skipping a beat, Brady would stick out his lip and insist, "I am *not* sorry!" And I'd think, *Well, we've got a ways to go here. Apparently, remorse is something of a learned response.*

When you think about it, remorse and humility are staples in the Christian faith. Each week, in the church my husband and I attend, we get on our knees to silently confess our sins. And then the congregation stands up to sing. Those are the two basic movements of the soul—we admit we continually fall short, and we celebrate God's grace. We receive his forgiveness.

Or think of the sacrament of Communion. You come forward or gather around a table with others—empty hands outstretched. The truth about you is spoken in public. The body and blood of Christ, given for you. Your need is spelled out—in fact, it's almost trumpeted.

We reenact this drama that puts our inadequacy and our sin in center stage before God and with each other, claiming together the mercy of God through his cross. If we're paying attention, the jig is up. There's no need to posture and pretend anymore. If we were truly shining stars and perfect people, we would not be gathered around this table. The sacrifice of Christ would not be necessary.

The body of Christ may be the only group you've ever belonged to where your deficiency—not your talents or your expertise—is what qualifies you for membership. The measure of our maturity is not how together we appear—but rather, the small moments when we are able to suffer the indignity of having our flaws and inadequacies exposed to someone we love. It's a peculiar grace, indeed.

Quite literally, the humility of owning our stuff breaks open the hard and frozen places in a close relationship—and God pours in the oil of his grace so that something new can happen.

Thank God, something new can happen.

We Need One Another

Sheila Walsh (*The Heartache No One Sees*)

One of my favorite books to read to my son at night is *Toot and Puddle: You Are My Sunshine* by Holly Hobbie. Toot and Puddle are two little pigs who are best friends. Previous books have detailed all sorts of wild adventures, but in this book Toot is in a bad place. Nothing that used to make him happy seems to touch him anymore. Puddle tries everything he can think of to restore a smile to his friend's face. He arranges a picnic and invites all their friends. It changes nothing. Puddle jumps through hoops trying to help his friend, but in the end only one thing makes a difference.

The thing that helps is that Puddle has stayed beside Toot through it all. Isn't that what we really long for deep in our souls, after all is said and done? We long for those who will stay with us for the rest of the journey on this earth. We need one another.

The Rewards of Being Known

Paula Rinehart (*Better Than My Dreams*)

Indeed, more is possible in relationships because of Christ. What we actually experience with each other, though, is directly proportional to the risks we are prepared to take. In other words, you don't get the chance to exhale—to find real places of safety and support in relationships—without taking a number of deep breaths. That sucking-in-air sensation is the way courage feels.

It takes a deep breath to put yourself out there in a friendship, doesn't it? Even in a marriage we can live as virtual strangers, unknown at any true depth.

Sometimes when I speak to women's groups, I ask a simple question. "When was the last time someone leaned across a table and said, 'So . . . how *are* you doing . . . I mean really?'" I see such longing on so many faces. Many of us lack anyone who knows us very well. Sometimes, though, the people who would ask a deeply personal question can't get past the parlor of our lives to ever see us with our hair down. We have not let ourselves be known.

I admit, though—that's no easy task. To share the truth of who we are feels like a risk because, indeed, it "may not gain us anything, we're afraid, but an uneasy silence and a fishy stare."[3] Or as Brennan Manning states in his own lively way:

Whom can I level with? To whom can I bare my soul? Whom dare I tell that I am benevolent and malevolent, chaste and randy, compassionate and vindictive, selfless and selfish, that beneath my brave words lives a frightened child . . . that I have blackened a friend's character, betrayed a trust, violated a confidence, that I am tolerant and thoughtful, a bigot and a blowhard, and that I really hate okra?[4]

There is always a risk in relationship—but it's a risk God means for us to take. I remember discussing this need with Chris, the woman who was addicted to prescription pain medication. She was determined to beat her problem on her own. She didn't want anyone to see her weakness.

"Then the body of Christ is useless to you," I offered in response. "You are missing the best part. Not everyone can handle where your life is. But God will give you a few trusted folks who will share your battle. You don't have to spend your life in hiding."

The love of Christ can heal us, truly. Yet most often, the love of Christ heals us through each other, as our shame is known. Perhaps that's why James includes this startling prescription for living the good life: "Confess your sins to each other and pray for each other so that you may be healed" (5:16 NIV).

That simple practice of humility is surprisingly powerful. Your need is out in the open, spoken in the presence of others—real, flesh-and-blood people who, by the modest act of hearing and praying, mirror the actual love and acceptance of God.

I sometimes think that these little moments strung together are really the primary way our souls are shaped. These moments are vastly underrated. It's like a story a friend recently shared with me. She's the quintessential mother who taught her four children to read—the kind of cookie-baking nurturer the rest of us wish we were. Only my friend has one daughter whose navel piercing and bad grades and rebellious attitude have nearly undone her. She is running out of patience. Every tactic she takes with her daughter seems to fail—it's so embarrassing. So my friend shared with a few people (none of whom had a difficult child) how at her wit's end she felt. She asked, simply, if they would pray for her.

We were talking later about how, strangely enough, this has helped. "How is it," she mused out loud, "that talking about how impossible I find it to love my daughter these days and then letting someone pray for me makes a difference? I don't understand, but in the oddest way, I've been more patient ever since."

We both shake our heads in wonder, really, at the way God applies such mysterious grace to the wounds of our souls through each other.

How hard do you find it to say to someone, "I'm struggling with this . . ." or "I feel like such a failure at that . . . Would you pray for me?" You don't want to miss what is available to you by staying glued to your mask. You want the body of Christ to be all God means for it to be in your life.

One scene in John's Gospel account is a window into how God makes us able to live boldly the life he has for us. It's a picture of what it means to experience Christ with each other so that our lives are actually transformed.

John devotes a great deal of space to this story. In fact, the details in John 21 are so specific you can practically taste the fish being cooked by the Sea of Galilee. The central character is Peter (who often manages to be the central character). The storyline is his failure—his huge, honking, glaring denial that he ever knew this man, Jesus, who was his Savior. Peter has returned to his day job as a fisherman. He has failed as a follower of Jesus—but at least, perhaps, he can still catch a few fish. Surely that much he can do.

The resurrected Christ appears by the Sea of Galilee after Peter has, once again, fished all night and caught nothing. Jesus steps right into the middle of all Peter's failure and shame. But this scene takes place with Peter among his closest friends. They know what Peter's done. They listen in on this conversation between Jesus and Peter, missing not a word.

Three times Jesus asks Peter if he loves him. Three times Peter insists that he does. And each time, Christ invites Peter to take that love and shepherd his sheep.

Wait a minute. Peter, who denied Christ when he most needed him, is going to be a shepherd of the early church? Who would believe that Christ would be so generous, so utterly gracious as to offer Peter his original place in the scheme of things? I wonder if Peter's friends choked on their fish as they watched.

When I consider the man Peter became and his role in the early church, I suspect that his power and boldness are directly connected to this scene. Peter does become the rock that Christ said he would be. He is utterly fearless—grateful, even, that his witness is bold enough to mark him by the authorities as a threat. Walking more than three thousand miles in his lifetime to share the gospel, Peter's influence transformed Asia Minor into the Christian corner of the Roman Empire.

Something life-changing happened for Peter among his friends. Perhaps his boldness is at least partially the result of having little else to hide. Peter experienced grace not unlike the way you and I must—as our failure and shame become known, in some small way, in the company of others who name his name and believe Christ is actually present in our midst.

The expression of transforming fellowship I know personally takes place not by the Sea of Galilee but under a North Carolina canopy of pine trees on various Sunday evenings. It's a collection of six couples who came together, innocently enough, in the beginning—when we still thought we had life by the tail. There were no glaring problems, no debilitating illnesses. We just met to share a portion of Scripture—to share our lives. What could be simpler?

Fifteen years have come and gone now. A lot has changed. We've weathered cancer treatments and struggling ministries, business reversals and children determined to sow their oats. Some evenings we show up hoping no one will ask what's happening in our lives—because even though they know, we'd rather not elaborate. It's better to simply pray about the obvious. Slowly, through the years, this fellowship has become its own kind of womb, nurturing this Christ-life within us—this Christ-life being poured out on many others.

There is a great gift in knowing people too well to successfully hide your flaws. Surely Peter experienced this. The polish wears off rather quickly when Jesus is present. Our group under the pine trees has been together a long time—long enough to disappoint each other occasionally. Yet we have chosen to hang together and let grace work its magic. In the oddest sort of way, the failure of our humanness makes the fellowship richer.

Perhaps nowhere in our journey of following Christ, past the rubble of broken dreams, do we stumble on any better gift—the sweet grace of being on that path with other folks. It's true—we are not what we will one day be. Yet God is generous. We taste his mercy even now through the forgiveness and encouragement we experience together. He gives us a few hands to hold along the way.

10

Living in Community

Why We Need Each Other

Stormie Omartian (*Finding Peace for Your Heart*)

While we were getting ready to go to someone's house for dinner, my husband, Michael, and I had a heated argument. We had misinterpreted each other's intentions and said words that were hurtful and pain provoking. I was reduced to tears and he to silence.

Great! I thought. *The last thing I want to do is be with other people feeling like this.* I silently ran through a list of reasons we could possibly cancel, but they sounded too feeble so I resigned myself to the evening.

We sat in silence during the entire drive to our host's home, except for Michael's asking, "Are you going to not speak to me all night?" To which I cleverly replied, "Are you going to not speak to *me* all night?"

I started thinking about the couple we were going to visit. Bob and Sally Anderson were one of the first Christian couples Michael and I befriended after we were married. We had a lot in common, including our children. Their daughter, Kristen, and our son, Christopher, were born about the same time and had become good friends. We loved being with them because they were solid in their relationship as well as their faith, and we knew there weren't going to be any weird surprises in store for us.

From the moment we arrived at their home I felt the tension between Michael and me dissipate. Throughout the evening our hearts softened, and by the time we went home we were laughing. It was as if the goodness of the Lord in the Anderson family had rubbed off on us and we were strengthened by it.

This kind of thing happened so many times that when our pastor exhorted us to "be in fellowship with other believers" and waved his hand across the congregation as if to get his sheep moving, I understood the need for it.

The word *fellowship* sounded weird and churchy the first time I heard it. It reminded me of tea and cookies after a missionary meeting or a potluck dinner in the church basement. I've since discovered it's much more than just coffee hour. Its dictionary definition is "companionship, a friendly association, mutual sharing, a group of people with the same interests." In the biblical sense, it's even more than that.

"Fellowship has to do with a mutuality in all parts of your life," our pastor taught us. "You bear one another's burdens and fulfill the law of Christ. You pray for one another when there is material need, you weep with those who weep and rejoice with those who rejoice. It's growing in an association with people who are moving in the same pathway you are and sharing with each other in your times of victory or need or your times of trial and triumph. It's growing in relationship."

I Get By with a Little Help from My Friends

Angela Thomas (*When Wallflowers Dance*)

The best reminders I have of my decision to choose an abundant, full life in Christ are my friends. I have some very cool friends who are at least ten giant steps ahead of me with God. They live wrapped up in the banner of his love. They consistently, tenderly, and firmly stand for God in all circumstances and through all manner of trials. Because they live intentionally, I am reminded.

I watch my friends intentionally parent in strength, and then I am reminded to parent the same. When my girlfriend intentionally takes on a new adventure, then I am motivated to find courage for my adventures. And when a friend talks to me about a new truth from God, good grief, I want to get in on that too!

It's virtually impossible to grow up without someone to talk to.

You may stop your life and begin to weed out the distractions. You may be at a great church. Intentional some days and connecting dots others. But I believe strongly that you are going to need someone beside you for these life lessons.

I have three friends who almost daily interact with me about my heart, the work God is doing, and my pursuit of spiritual truth. One is Dennis, who lives on the other side of the country. My two girlfriends also live far away. We spend time together a few times a year, so most of our friendship happens by phone. I have a counselor here in town, my pastor, and lots of great friends, but these mentoring, discipling friends just don't live close.

I want to tell you more about Dennis, so you'll have a better picture of the kind of person I'm talking about. Dennis is going to love that I'm telling you he's in his early fifties. About ten years ahead of me. He pastors a church in Southern California where he and his wife serve with the purest hearts for ministry I have ever known. This guy has a great, big love for people, and he desperately wants them to have a healthy, growing relationship with God. He is not afraid of broken lives or messy people or the wild stories they bring into his office. He's a lot like Jesus that way.

I have watched him consistently pursue God for the past twenty years. I have watched him walk through trials and heartache with great integrity. I have heard about the disappointments he has faced, and yet his heart toward God remains tender. He could accumulate stuff, but instead, he and Karen give their stuff away and their time away and their hearts away over and over. He could work harder at remaining comfortable, but I keep watching him jump into the trenches no one wants to be in.

There were days in my darkest hours when I talked to Dennis every few hours. He said, "If you need another breath, just call me. We'll talk until you can breathe." We started at learning to breathe again, and now he thinks it's the coolest thing that I'm really dancing with God.

We speak at least once a week now. I talked to him yesterday. I run career decisions past him. He doesn't know anything about publishing, but he knows a lot about the heart. He keeps me true to my heart. I get ministry advice and parenting advice. But mostly, Dennis points me to Jesus. Consistent. Unswerving. Faithful. Come to Jesus; come to Jesus.

I want you to have someone who will consistently say the name of Jesus to you and for you and over you. I want you to be able to lean into the strength of another. Remember, healing doesn't happen in the dark. Your healing and maturing will happen inside the context of strong relationship. When a strong woman of God steps into your life, she brings the light of Christ with her.

Maybe you don't think you have a Dennis anywhere in your life. Maybe not yet. You have been made for friendship and companionship. You and I grow because of those relationships. God knows all of that, and I believe with all my heart that he will provide for you. You must pray and begin to consciously seek that person.

It Is Good, but It Is Not Always Easy

Sheila Walsh (*God Has a Dream for Your Life*)

I am a big fan of the Special Olympics. Having spent a summer volunteering in a home for mentally challenged adults, I have great respect for those with intellectual disabilities; they are much stronger and braver than most of us.

The Special Olympics' commitment to sports training and competition offers wonderful opportunities to those who are excluded from many traditional events. It allows them to experience the joy of bringing all you have to the table, of showing courage and being part of a sporting community.

The first International Special Olympics Summer Games were held on July 20, 1968. Eunice Kennedy Shriver officially opened the games with these inspiring words: "In ancient Rome, the gladiators went into the arena with these words on their lips: 'Let me win, but if I cannot win, let me be brave in the attempt' . . . Today, all of you young athletes are in the arena. Many of you will win, but even more important, I know you will be brave and bring credit to your parents and to your country."

The games are always uplifting, but there was one track-and-field event that I will never forget: the 100-meter race. Early in the race, a young athlete tripped and fell. He hit the track hard. The crowd gasped as they watched him tumble and cry out. Then the most amazing thing happened.

The other athletes looked back to see what had happened. When they saw the boy face down on the track, one by one they turned around and went to his aid. That day, hand in hand, all the runners crossed the finish line as one. It was quite a sight.

Can you imagine anything like that happening apart from the community that we call mentally challenged? It was one of the most inspiring and humbling events I've ever seen. All I could think as I watched with tears on my cheeks and cheers in my heart was, *That's how we are supposed to be as the body of Christ!*

One of the most profound experiences for me over the last few years has been to see the way God uses pain as a bridge to connect women. When we struggle with anything that is shame-based, it can isolate us and cut us off from what we need most: companionship and comfort.

Patsy Clairmont jokes from the Women of Faith conference stage about how hard it can be for women to cheer each other on. "You hear that a friend has been promoted at work or someone else in the choir gets the solo and you say, 'I'm so happy for you,' while privately you're thinking, *She makes me sick!*"

Jealousy can eat at our hearts like a foul cancer. It distracts us from experiencing the dream that God has for each of us. The root of jealousy is fear: fear that someone else is more loved or more accepted than we are.

The apostle Paul addressed this issue briefly in his letter to the church at Philippi. The beginnings of the Philippian church, where a small group of women met by the water to worship is written about in Acts. Lydia and her family gave their lives to Christ, and many other women followed.

The church began to grow, but trouble was brewing: two of the prominent women in the church, Euodia and Syntyche, could not get along. Not much is written about the dispute, but the fact that Paul felt compelled to include it in his letter to the church at Philippi is significant. He says, "I implore Euodia and I implore Syntyche to be of the same mind in the Lord" (Phil. 4:2 NKJV). I can't imagine how humiliating it would be to show up in such a significant letter from Paul to the entire church family in Philippi.

The women in Philippi loved and honored Paul. It is thought most likely that Euodia and Syntyche were of the same class of women as Lydia, women who underwrote much of Paul's work for the gospel. Part of his letter is his deep gratitude for all they have done for him. Now he writes from prison and begs these two women to put their differences aside for the sake of the kingdom.

As I read the letter, I wonder why Paul didn't write a separate note just to the women in question. Was Paul merely putting two difficult women in their places? Did he intend to embarrass them into behaving? I don't think so at all. The note in the book of Philippians is there because God wanted it there. Many of Paul's letters contained instruction to a fledgling church on how to handle problems among believers.

Rather than dishonoring these two women, Paul was indicating how crucial these women were to the work of the Lord. He goes on to say, "And I urge you also, true companion, help these women who labored with me in the gospel" (4:3 NKJV). The Greek word used here for "labored" is a strong one. It calls up the picture of gladiators fighting side by side for victory. Paul is urging the believers in Philippi to put aside their differences, which are small in light of the gospel of Christ.

The tone of Paul's letter to the church in Philippi shows how much these women have blessed and encouraged him. As a brother he is urging them—not knowing how long he has left on this earth— to rise above whatever is tearing them apart. That is true love.

We all get caught up in petty differences that can get blown out of proportion. Sometimes we are so stubborn that we back ourselves into a corner and can't get out. Paul, in love, is saying in essence, "Come on, girls; you are better than this. Don't let the enemy spoil what God wants to do here." It's a reminder that we often need.

We will never be able to get along with one another on our own. But the great news is that we aren't asked to do it on our own. It is the life and love of Christ himself that gives us strength to do the things that are impossible for us when left to our own abilities.

Paul rejoices in Christ as the source of our strength:

Does your life in Christ give you strength? Does his love comfort you? Do we share together in the spirit? Do you have mercy and kindness? If so, make me very happy by having the same thoughts, sharing the same love, and having one mind and purpose. When you do things, do not let selfishness or pride be your guide. Instead, be humble and give more honor to others than to yourselves. Do not be interested only in your own life, but be interested in the lives of others. (Phil. 2:1–4 NCV)

Make Every Effort
Angela Thomas (*A Beautiful Offering*)

Confession hasn't ever been one of my best things.

Hiding sin? I have done that.

Standing quietly instead of owning my faults? Yep, I've done that too.

Repairing broken relationships? It was sometimes easier to pretend that nothing was broken.

Last week I was running errands like a wild woman, and just as I was about to hop out of the car at the post office, I turned on the radio long enough to hear a man quote from the book of Hebrews. He said, "Make every effort to live in peace with all men (12:14 NIV)."

That's all I heard; I turned it off and kept plowing through my list.

A little while later, I was waiting at an intersection when a woman I have known for the past few years drove up beside me. Either she didn't see me or she chose not to look at me, but either way, my seeing her was a poignant reminder. I had been in a friendship with her that didn't end so well. I never quite knew where she went or why.

It's amazing how God uses the powerful words of Scripture to stop us dead in our tracks and rearrange our thoughts. Just after I had spotted my withdrawn friend, my head began screaming, *Angela, you are not at peace with that woman and you have to do something about it. Make every effort, remember?*

Not always so quick to obey the promptings of the Holy Spirit, I went to the grocery store and then to the bank, but God wouldn't leave me alone. I was pretty sure that he wanted me to call this woman I hadn't talked to in six months. My stomach hurt while I punched her number into my cell phone. Some days, obedience makes you feel nauseated.

She answered and the conversation went something like this:

"Hello."

"Hey, this is Angela." I tried to muster up some confidence.

"Oh," she said. I knew immediately this wasn't going to be good, but I went for it anyway.

"I'm calling because I just saw you at an intersection about an hour ago, and I felt stupid. I'm calling to see if there is anything I can do to help things between us end differently or better. I don't want to feel stupid the rest of my life, so can we talk about what happened? Can we talk about what didn't happen? Could I say anything or listen in a way that would help?"

"I didn't see you at an intersection," she offered without emotion.

"That's okay, I just want things to be different between us. I want us to be at peace."

"Well, I'm on my way to my son's football game. I didn't see that it was you when I answered the phone. I thought it was some-body else."

"Sounds like I've caught you at a bad time," I said, feeling triple stupid.

"Yeah, gotta go."

"Okay, bye."

Click. No good-bye. No "I'll call you back." No hope that this will ever be straightened out. I could have just about run to the bathroom and lost it. I felt sicker than before I called. And I wasn't too happy with God either.

I mean, I have enough stress. Grayson has a project due with modeling clay and I am not crafty. I have to figure out how to send my taxes to the federal government next month. The hall upstairs needs painting. Every kid in this house needs winter uniforms for school. I haven't spent enough time with the friends that I love, and I've been meaning to bake a pie for my neighbors for two years. Good night. There is enough pressure and guilt in my life to last me decades. I did not need to hear the disheartening voice of a woman who is cold toward me. It ruined my day. What was God doing? And what was I thinking?

I was thinking about the Hebrews verse and Matthew 5:23–24, and I was thinking that if I could reconcile with that woman, then it would bless God.

So what now, God? Okay, I remembered someone who had a grudge against me, and I went to her. It was obviously a bust. What do I do with the offering of my life if I have left it at the altar and gone to be reconciled, but she was unwilling? You know, I've tried with her before. I don't think she's coming around anytime soon. So do I just stand here biding my time, waiting for the offering of my life to be acceptable when she changes her heart? Tell me what to do with this verse. Tell me where to go from here.

Maybe you can tell that I was a little miffed with the prompting to call an angry woman. I felt like screaming, "I want my life to be a beautiful offering to you, but I don't know what to do with this!" I think I prayed. I probably whined.

But here is the lesson I believe God gave to me:

First, *acknowledge your sin to yourself and to God.* When you and I remember that there is someone who has a grudge against us, it is our responsibility to own the part we play in the disagreement, misunderstanding, or conflict.

Second, *move toward the person.* We can hide, cover, or run from our responsibility in relationships for the rest of our lives. But God is calling us, very specifically in these verses, to move toward the one who is offended or hurt or misunderstood.

Third, *go immediately.* That means pretty soon. You know, right after it has come to your mind. Waiting three years is not immediately.

My daughter was in the car with me and she had just had an encounter that was difficult. I said, "Call that person right now and try to make it right."

She said, "I don't know if I can."

"I know it stinks, but one of the characteristics of a Christian is that we try to resolve quickly," I offered.

"Did you just make that up?" she asked.

"Jesus made it up and said, 'As you go, look like this.'"

"Sometimes this is hard," she mumbled as she reached for her cell phone.

"Most of the time, this one is hard for Mom too."

Days went by and I continued to reflect on my desire to live this verse with my grumpy friend. I decided that I had followed the instruction, even though reluctantly. We just didn't get to the reconciled part. And honestly, unless she comes to a softer place, there might not ever be reconciliation. I felt so stuck about what to do with my offering. Can I still bring it to God if we don't ever reconcile?

Then I remembered the Hebrews passage on the radio that had initially prompted my call. The writer had said, "Make every effort." When I put these divine words from God together, then I get,

Make every effort to acknowledge your own sin.

Make every effort to move toward the injustice.

Make every effort to reconcile immediately.

That's all we can do. Make every effort to honor the words of Jesus. Check your own heart. Respond in obedience. And then rest.

Standing in the Gap—Praying for One Another
Sheila Walsh (*Get Off Your Knees and Pray*)

Each morning after breakfast in the psychiatric ward, my new friends and I would meet in the patients' lounge, join hands in a circle, and pray for one another. For the first few days I couldn't pray, but I was deeply moved by those who prayed for me.

- "Dear Father, help Sheila today to find the courage to face the truth about her life knowing that you love her."
- "Dear Father, help her to face her fear and not to be afraid to cry."
- "Dear Father, thank you for bringing her to a safe place. Help her to feel safe today."

I cannot tell you what those simple, profound prayers meant to me. After all the years I had lived as a believer, for the first time I began to experience what it feels like to be part of the body of Christ. And soon I was able to offer my own prayers for my companions— simple, perhaps halting, but heartfelt. And I could see that my prayers for them were gratefully received too. Looking back over my life, I can't believe I spent so long trying to impress people with my prayers, as if I were applying for a job! Prayer is not supposed to put walls between us; it is supposed to break them down. Over and over in the New Testament, we are encouraged to pray for each other:

- Make this your common practice: Confess your sins to each other and pray for each other so that you can live together whole and healed. The prayer of a person living right with God is something powerful to be reckoned with. (James 5:16–17 MSG)
- Every time you cross my mind, I break out in exclamations of thanks to God. Each exclamation is a trigger to prayer. I find myself praying for you with a glad heart. (Phil. 1:3–4 MSG)

- And pray for us, too, that God may open a door for our message, so that we may proclaim the mystery of Christ, for which I am in chains. (Col. 4:3 NIV)

Only when I was broken enough to put aside my rehearsed prayers was I truly able to experience what a joy it is to pray for others—to think of something and someone else. And to feel how prayers impacted not only others but me.

God has always called us to walk out our faith as a people—not as individuals but as a group. When he called the Israelites out of Egypt, he called them to come out together, not one by one. The Psalms were written as corporate liturgy to be sung together as a community. Jesus told us that he is returning for a bride, who is all of us in the body of Christ.

This means that not only is prayer our personal means of communication with God but also it is a way for us believers to come together as one. Never, ever underestimate the power of praying together. The Bible tells us:

- Take this most seriously: A yes on earth is yes in heaven; a no on earth is no in heaven. What you say to one another is eternal. I mean this. When two of you get together on anything at all on earth and make a prayer of it, my Father in heaven goes into action. And when two or three of you are together because of me, you can be sure that I'll be there. (Matt. 18:18–20 MSG)

- Through the Spirit they urged Paul not to go on to Jerusalem. But when our time was up, we left and continued on our way. All the disciples and their wives and children accompanied us out of the city, and there on the beach we knelt to pray. (Acts 21:4–5 NIV)

- Everything in the world is about to be wrapped up, so take nothing for granted. Stay wide-awake in prayer. Most of all, love each other as if your life depended on it. Love makes up for practically anything. (1 Peter. 4:7–8 MSG)

I hope you've had the opportunity to truly pray in a communal experience. If not, I encourage you to give yourself that gift. There is nothing like it. As I experienced with my fellow patients, it is fellowship at its barest and most powerful. And it is life changing. For me, the closest relationships I have are the friends I pray with. Prayer is acknowledging the invisible in the presence of the visible, and I believe the evil one trembles when he sees God's people on their knees together.

Growing, Together

Paula Rinehart (*Better Than My Dreams*)

Strolling through a small country store, I stumbled on a painted sign that summarized the plainest truth about relationships I've seen in one sentence.

Sometimes you are the pigeon—and sometimes you are the statue.

Can it be said any more succinctly? If we want our lives uncluttered and free of drama, then we need to find a hillside and camp out alone. Real relationships are messy. They inevitably bring a share of pigeon droppings. Sometimes you are the one who feels dumped on—and other times, you're the pigeon doing the dumping, and someone else feels the impact.

There are sophisticated ways of saying this, of course. The best one is that we are all both victims and agents. To live together as fallen people, on the far side of Eden, means that we hurt each other, and we are hurt by each other—often in nearly equal measure. No one's hands are clean. Letting that reality touch you deeply will bring something wonderful—it's what the Bible calls "humility of mind." Here is the way the apostle Paul writes about it:

> Do nothing from selfishness or empty conceit, but with humility
> of mind regard one another as more important than yourselves;
> do not merely look out for your own personal interests, but also
> for the interests of others. (Phil. 2:3–4 NASB)

A dose of humility goes a long way in a friendship or a marriage. It's the hidden ticket to nearly everything we call real in a relationship.

Henri Nouwen once said that true Christian community is not like having a circle of friends—because true community always includes someone we don't like. She grates on our nerves. She reminds me of my weakness. I would not pick her for a friend, really, and yet, *voila!* God has put her in my life. That is the gift, actually. In a context of grace, I am reminded of my own neediness and failure, and thereby humility opens me to receive from God as he touches my life through other people.

Experiencing the grace of Christ makes true relationship with each other possible. But make no mistake. The mess and the grace are present with each other at the same time, perhaps more than we bargained for. There will be moments that call for painful apology and others that look like scary confrontation. We won't be in any relationship long before our selfishness starts to show—or real sacrifice is called for.

If we ever grow up, we will have to grow up together.

11

Shining Your Light

The Salt and Light Phenomenon

Angela Thomas (*A Beautiful Offering*)

My kids go to a Christian school. We hang out with a lot of believers at Bible studies and church. My best friends are a very cool medley of godly men and women. And just about every other weekend I get on a plane to spend a couple of days with a bunch of women who love Jesus. All in all, my family is surrounded by Christians, all the time, almost everywhere we go. I'm not sure if it's the best balance of Christ and the world, but it's how it is for now.

A few months ago I went to a barbecue with one of my children. It was supposed to be a party, I guess. Family by family these people came, out of breath, late, apologizing, grumbling, and carrying a tray of something for the big hoopla. There were all those fake smiles that we pass around at parties Christians come to. Polite conversation without depth or heart. No music. Heaven forbid, no dancing. And miserably, no laughing either. I was just about to die.

So I decided to become the life of the party. It's not my natural role because I am not a true extrovert. But we obviously didn't have any takers that night, and I was going to have to be the entertainment. Let me tell you something, when you try to make people laugh after they have decided in their hearts that nothing in the whole wide world is funny anymore, it's painful. I just wanted to get my kid and my bowl of pasta salad and go home.

I bombed as the vaudeville act, and so I asked Jesus, "Why am I here? This is pitiful. My child is playing with friends, and I am stuck with their dreary Christian parents." I felt as if he told me to pay attention to the women and especially to look into their eyes.

I took my mission seriously and tried to interact with every woman there. I wanted to look beneath the surface of politeness and find out what God wanted to show me. I asked each one a few questions and worked the barbecue the rest of the night. All the women were younger than I, late twenties and early thirties. All of them were tired and burdened. I don't know if one marriage in the room was good, much less great. What came to the surface over the course of the evening was a theme that linked each of these women together. The one thing that I believe God wanted me to see was that every one of those women appeared to have given up.

In her own way, each woman had either gone numb or gone

away or gone under. They had stopped calling for help. Stopped trying to figure anything out. Stopped caring what they looked like or sounded like. Timid. Fearful. Guilt-laden. Sad and incredibly without passion. I found myself in a house full of believers desperately without salt and light.

There is a phenomenon here in the city of Knoxville. It's called football at the University of Tennessee. I didn't grow up here, and I didn't go to school here, so I don't even know if I can explain to you what happens in this city every fall. People turn orange. I am not kidding. Nobody looks good in that color, not one person I've ever met, but they don't care. Every person in this town wears orange on Friday and Saturday. They fly orange flags on top of their cars and outside their homes. They hang orange-and-white pom-poms from the trunk or the rearview mirror. They paint things orange and grow orange flowers and buy orange beanbag chairs sold along the side of the road. It's crazy.

Yesterday was the first football game of this season. I promise you, I think I was the only person who did not go to the game or stay inside to watch it on TV. I drove to the store and it felt as though I'd missed the Rapture. With 110,000 people at the stadium and everyone else glued to a big screen, this city was empty. No cars on the street. No one shopping. It was weird. They even closed the pool in my neighborhood all day yesterday because of the game. These people are wild and fun and very serious about their football.

Everywhere I'll go for the next few months they'll be talking about the team—make that the only team that matters. They will be so excited that I'll get excited and I'll be talking about football too. I even watched the coach's postgame show this morning because I wanted to catch the highlights and know which plays we'll be discussing this coming week. The enthusiasm is contagious and it lures you in. They make me want to love what they love. I want to go to one of those big parties called a UT game. I might even want to look awful in orange just to be like one of them.

This phenomenon called Tennessee football is salty. It makes everyone who tastes it thirst for more. The orange-colored light called Volunteer-love shines brightly around here. The whole city is attracted to its brilliance, and we instinctively move toward the allure of its glow.

So here's my question: Why was the Jesus party with the Jesus people so boring? And why are the Tennessee fans alive and passionate about the ones they love? Something is not adding up here. The UT thing is fun, but it's fleeting. Win today. Yippee. Lose next week. Too bad. But the Jesus thing is eternal. Did anybody hear that? Eternal! And the Jesus thing heals wounded souls and broken hearts. Really, is anybody listening? Call in the marching band. Cue the cheerleaders. We've got even more reason than they do for a celebration. When the Jesus people show up, others should know that tenderness and acceptance just walked into the room. They should be able to "feel" a difference in our spirit and the way we interact. We should make them thirsty for Jesus and the truth of his compassion and forgiveness. We have the opportunity to give Light where they have known only darkness.

Blah, blah, blah. I bet you've heard all this before.

But if you've heard it all before, then why don't our lives look more like orange people for Jesus? When did we stop believing in the power of the Son of God? Why don't our eyes reflect the joy of his presence? How can we withhold compassionate acceptance when Jesus invited everyone to come to him?

No wonder my neighbors would rather go to the UT game than come to church with me. I kind of understand. Sometimes I'd rather go to the game than hang out with the pretenders and the perpetually downcast. Sometimes it seems easier to cheer for a first down than to cheer for lives redeemed. One time I'd like to show up for church, yell all the words to the fight song, do the wave with my best friends, and cheer for the Jesus victory in people's lives. I know, it sounds wacky. Maybe it's outside your box. God is holy and deserves our reverence. He is and he does. But where have all the salty people gone? Where is the light of the world?

I just don't think we look like what he had in mind. Jesus said, *As you go, be like salt, and as you go, take my light into the world.* I'm not sure what happened to a lot of us. I think maybe we gave up.

A Vision, a Passion, a Mission

Jill Briscoe (*A Woman and Her God*)

Jesus had a vision, a passion, and a mission. Those are the three words I want us to consider, because women can be involved in a ministry with a vision, a passion, and a mission. Consider Jesus and the Samaritan woman. God delighted in taking the least, the lost, and the last—like this woman—and using them. How quickly did the Samaritan woman understand his heart, his purpose, and his mission! The woman at the well, I believe, represents women everywhere—women who are forgiven sinners and women who are unforgiven sinners. Which describes you? The Samaritan woman was unforgiven, just like a lot of women in the world. But then she encountered Jesus.

So the Samaritan woman is about to have grace enter her life through this man at the well, this man who sees her need. Even though he is thirsty and hungry and tired, when he meets her, his passion and vision for a lost soul take center stage. And where are the disciples at this time? I think they represent church people. They are disciples of Jesus, convinced he's the Messiah, having left everything to follow him, but they are mostly focused on their lunch. They represent us, quite honestly. They can't take their eyes off material possessions and focus on spiritual realities, including things God has asked them to do in this world. So they've walked into town to buy bread. When the disciples return, they're surprised to find Jesus talking to a Samaritan woman. Finally, she departs, leaving her water jug with Jesus. At this point, the disciples offer him lunch.

"Rabbi, eat something," they say.

"I have food to eat you don't know anything about," he explains.

"Did somebody bring him lunch?" they ask, looking around.

"Did he eat her lunch? Well, who brought him lunch?" How frustrated Jesus must have been with the disciples! For that matter, how frustrated he must be with us when we can't take our focus off lunch. Our vision is so limited. The problem is, if we become comfortable in our faith, we tend to become self-satisfied and then we don't even care if the world's gone to hell in a handbasket. We have no vision and certainly no passion.

But Jesus had a driving passion for the harvest fields. Look at John 4:35: "Open your eyes and look at the fields! They are ripe for harvest" (NIV). What was he looking at just then? He was looking down the hill toward the village. He was seeing all the villagers coming to him in their long, white robes, winding their way up the hill. And they must have looked like sheaves of wheat walking. And Jesus said, "Look, open your eyes. Look at the fields ready for harvest. How can you think of food at a time like this?"

If you have a vision for the lost, you tend to lose your appetite because your vision leads to passion. Suddenly your stomach becomes tied in knots. Let me ask you something: When was the last time your stomach ached over a lost soul? Take a good look at the people around you. Just as it was in biblical times, the fields are ripe. It's harvest time! Proverbs 10:5 says a son who sleeps during a harvest is a disgrace to his father. Remember, the harvest field is ripe. Certainly in America there are sheaves all over the place, thirsty sheaves longing for a drink of Living Water, not knowing even how to ask for it. "Gather me into God's barn," their souls cry out. But we are so focused on our own lives, we can't take our eyes off our lunch.

Meanwhile, Jesus was driven to do the will of God as revealed in the Word of God. When we're intent on doing the will of God and fulfilling his purpose for our lives, then we are going to discover his will. And his will is revealed in the Word of God. It's right there, for you and me. God's plan for our lives is to come alongside those who do not know him. That's a privilege. It's exciting!

Thirty years ago, when I first started to reach out to women through a women's ministry program, there was simply one group of women. I started a Bible study with six women and it eventually grew to eight hundred. I stood up, taught the Scriptures, and then went home. But things have changed. Women are more like tribes now. There's a tribe of young mothers, there's a tribe of widows, there's a tribe of women who work outside the home, and there's a tribe of divorced women. Each tribe has its own culture, language, dress, thought process, and needs. What attracts a young mother will not necessarily attract a widow or a divorced woman. To reach women, we often have to understand their contemporary culture. For example, what is life like for a divorced woman who feels rejected? And do we understand the young mother who is happily married, trying to raise godly children? She is a world apart from the divorced woman. We have to do our homework if we're ever going to reach the lost.

And this is what Jesus did with the woman at the well. He knew what to say, and he knew how to say it. His vision led to passion. "Oh, if you only knew," he said. And eventually she did.

And this led to a mission. What else would you call it when the Samaritan woman won a city to Christ? She was a brand-new believer. Do you have to attend a seminary or Bible college before you can win your whole town to Christ? Absolutely not! You can start as soon as you believe.

Years ago when the girl in the hospital bed next to me led me to Christ, she said, "Now, Jill, everybody who comes to your bedside is going to hear what you did today."

"They are?" I asked.

"Yes," she said.

"Who's going to tell them?"

"You are."

"What do I tell them?"

"Tell them what you just did. Tell them about our conversation."

"Who am I going to tell?" I asked.

"Everybody who comes to your bedside. Look! There's a nurse coming. Start with her."

And so I did. And that day there were not a few people who heard me explain in a stumbling, awkward manner who Christ is.

Now it's your turn. You are a woman Jesus loves and calls to minister to the lost. Start your ministry. Just start right where you are. The mission field is literally between your own two feet at any given time.

Becoming the Light of the World

Angela Thomas (*A Beautiful Offering*)

Right after Jesus proclaimed that we are the salt of the earth, he said,

> You are the light of the world. A city on a hill cannot be hidden. Neither do people light a lamp and put it under a bowl. Instead they put it on its stand, and it gives light to everyone in the house. In the same way, let your light shine before men, that they may see your good deeds and praise your Father in heaven. (Matt. 5:14–16 NIV)

Over in John 8:12, Jesus said of himself,

> I am the light of the world. Whoever follows me will never walk in darkness, but will have the light of life. (NIV)

It's clear from the Sermon on the Mount passage that the life of a believer is like a lamp or a candle. We cannot *be* the light in ourselves, we can only reflect to a dark and dying world the light that we have received from the Lord Jesus. Paul said in 2 Corinthians,

> God . . . has flooded our hearts with his light. We now can enlighten men only because we can give them knowledge of the glory of God, as we see it in the face of Jesus Christ. (4:6 PHILLIPS)

As I see it, there are a couple of poignant applications for us to take from this call to brightness:

A brilliant light is the result of a deeper walk with Jesus. We cannot fake some light for Jesus, although many, including me, have tried. We will not shine like a city on a hill without a close fellowship with God. Because we have an intimate relationship with Jesus, "we see the face of Christ," and then God comes through that intimacy to flood our hearts with his light.

I have spoken to this before, but a brilliant light comes from more than just showing up at church or another study. Please don't hear me as knocking church; it can happen there, but it isn't automatic. Becoming the light of the world involves a thirsty, righteous pursuit of the person and heart of Christ.

Pursuing light gets messy. And it's tiring and sometimes nobody around you gets it. And you keep growing and running while everyone else seems to be spiritually lounging in a hammock, sipping a fruit smoothie, trying to forget the reason they're here. This deeper-walk thing is the only way into greater light. The faint of heart give up. The whiners take their toys and go home. The crybabies blame everybody else for their lack of light.

Becoming the light of the world means knowing the Light of the World. Seeking the Light of the World. Basking in the Light of the World. You have to get up and get serious and do whatever it takes to get yourself out of the shadows and into the overwhelming, eye-squinting glare of his presence. God is waiting to make you into a brilliant light, but you have to move toward him in relationship.

The light of Christ in you is not to be hidden. Some Sundays at my church there is so much light in the room that I think we should be able to replace the power grid for our entire city. If that is happening at churches all over the country, then why is the light of Christ so dim in this world? Why is it dark out there? Why are people fumbling their way through empty lives, satisfied with the fleeting strike of a match, when instead they could have the radiance of the Son?

We don't see the reflection of Jesus because people take their light home and hide it. We can sing, "I'm gonna let it shine," all day long and then go right out to the car and snuff it out. What are we so afraid of? Why are we afraid that they'll see Jesus in us? Do we fear not knowing what to say? What to do?

I say to my kids all the time, "Take it to the hoop." They know that basketball term means, "Don't just do a job halfway. Take your dirty clothes all the way to the laundry room. Rinse your plate and put it in the dishwasher too. Clear everything off the table, not just part of it. All the way to the hoop, baby."

I could say to us as the light of Christ, "Be the city." Don't settle for being a twenty-watt bulb, hidden away in some useless closet in the basement, when you can be as luminous as the morning sun breaking through the darkness of night. Don't worry about what to say or do or how to respond. The Light-giver will supply every need. Just be the city, baby. Shine the truth of Jesus with everything you've got, and he will focus and refine and disburse your light for his glory.

God seems to be redefining what *shine* means to me. It used to mean quietly speaking into people's lives with Scripture and modeling for them the heart of the Father, as best I knew how. As I continue to mature in Christ, *shine* is coming to include a compassionate boldness that I never knew I could possess. As I become more and more convinced of the truths of God, I am able to give them out boldly. I hear myself speaking in strength to unbelievers, not ashamed of my calling or my Savior. I find myself entering into difficult situations, realizing fully that I am responsible to bring the light of Christ into the room. Through the years and through our relationship, God seems to be turning up the light that he has set within me. Watch and see how he does the same for you.

When you shine, then people get to see the Father. It's true. When folks have been sitting in the dark or hanging around in murky places with dark-hearted people, it's obvious when the light of Christ shows up. God loves it when you and I step into the pitch-black night of this world with the candle of his presence. There is a path to the Father, and your light shows the way.

Jesus said to be salt and light. It's pleasing to him. It demonstrates to the world to whom you belong. The salty and the light-bearers are becoming a beautiful offering with their lives.

But maybe you haven't made anyone thirsty lately, and maybe your light has almost gone out. Here is the grace of his calling to me and to you:

It's never too late to become.
It's never too late to change.

You haven't been away too long.

His forgiveness can still cover your sin.

His love can heal your wounds.

Your life isn't too broken for him.

As long as you have breath, it's never too late with Jesus.

He doesn't expect your offering to be perfect. He never said that
it would be easy. Move toward him, and watch him super-
naturally make you into salt and light.

Stay the path.

Let him pick you up when you've fallen.

Face in his direction.

You may have given up on God, but he has never given up
on you.

Go be the city, baby. Go be the salt.

Spend It All

Angela Thomas (*A Beautiful Offering*)

My offering is meager and tarnished, but oh, how I desire that it
become beautiful. Will you hear Jesus say, *As you go . . . be like me*,
and then respond with your life? The life that is in front of us can be
more beautiful than we could have dreamed. You have more love to
return to God than you could have imagined.

A few weeks ago my pastor told of two races on a Saturday.
That morning his wife ran a 5k through their neighborhood. He

stood in the driveway with his coffee and cheered on his bride. In the afternoon, their daughter ran cross-country for her high school. This time the whole family stood at the finish line and cheered her start and her victory. He said that at both races, he heard himself yelling for his girls, "Spend it all!"

Life is a journey. Sometimes a race and sometimes a crawl. You can hold back and hesitate. You can live in fear and respond half-heartedly. But would you decide to give everything you have for the glory of God? There is nothing to hoard, because God replenishes so freely. There is no reason to resist or question his love. God has already proved that he's wild about you.

Lift up your eyes this day and fix your gaze on the One who calls you beautiful. Determine in your heart that you will return his love with your life. Do whatever it takes. Spare no expense. Run with the whole of your energies into the arms of your Beloved.

Spend it all, my friend. Spend it all.

12

Remembering
You Are Chosen

You Are Chosen

Sheila Walsh (*Let Go*)

I will never forget the night I was baptized in my home church in Ayr, Scotland. I was sixteen years old, and there were several of us being baptized. We filed into the church and sat in the front row, which had been reserved for us. As the first hymn began to play, I started to weep. I couldn't stop. I was overwhelmed with an awareness that I was doing something Jesus had asked me to do, and in that very act of obedience his presence and his delight seemed so tangible.

When it was time for the baptisms, we made our way to the stairs at the side of the baptismal tank. One by one, each person climbed the stairs and went down into the water. When it was my turn, I was shaking so much I could hardly get down the other side. I stood in the water as Pastor Gunn took my hand. Before he baptized me, he said, "Sheila, I asked the Lord for a verse for you and he gave me this: 'You did not choose me but I chose you. And I appointed you to go and bear fruit, fruit that will last, so that the Father will give you whatever you ask him in my name'" (John 15:16 NRSV).

With that, he lowered me into the water.

When I came up, it was all I could do not to shout and dance (which is hard to do with a soaking wet robe clinging to you). I felt as if I had been kissed by God.

God chose me. I couldn't get that wonderful truth out of my heart. No one had ever chosen me before. I wasn't good at sports, so if anyone was asked by our gym teacher to pick a team, I was always at the bottom. When the boys had to pick a partner to practice for the school dance when I was sixteen years old, I had to wait for quite some time as the last few reluctant and awkward boys took what was left.

Chosen by God . . . now I just had to work out what that meant. Did it mean that from this point on in my life everything would fit neatly into place? Did it mean all my imperfections would be perfected? I'm a little embarrassed by this admission now, but I even wondered if perhaps, as I came out of the water that night, I would be changed. I thought it possible that my skin might have cleared up and I might have left a few unwanted pounds in the water.

I wanted an outward expression of an inner truth. Surely if God chose me, then he might want to make life a little easier for me. I guess I thought that being a "new creation" would show up on the surface (2 Cor. 5:17). If I was leaving my old self in the water symbolically and being raised to a new life, then maybe I would look "new" on the outside.

I have come to understand that what Jesus wanted was to live his life in and through me, not to fulfill a few teenage dreams that might have changed my outer appearance but done nothing for my heart. Jesus was inviting me to join him in a dance that would take me through all the seasons of life.

Destiny is hard to define by our culture's standards. We look at a boy who handles a football well and think, *He's a natural-born athlete.* We look at a girl whose beauty is striking and think, *Her looks will take her far.* Our destiny as believers is not so easily defined or short-lived. When I came up out of the baptismal waters, I looked for a change on my face, but God was working a change in my heart to see his hand in all the circumstances of life. That is God's gift to you at this moment. You are chosen and loved. Your future is safe and secure, bought with the precious blood of Christ. You may not feel like a princess most days, but that does not change the truth that you are.

You Have a Part to Play

Paula Rinehart (*Better Than My Dreams*)

Of all the ways the sovereignty of God affects how we see life, how we interpret our story is perhaps the most foundational. Often, the very things we call meaningless detours in our journey turn out to be the path we were supposed to be traveling. We have come home—but by a road we would not have known to choose.

I think of a conversation with a talented woman named Sylvia, who sees her life as something of a failure. Her labeling felt unusual to me, since it was clear that the woman I was talking to was both capable and accomplished.

"You don't understand," she corrected me with a note of exasperation. "I am midway through my thirties and just now discovering something I want to pursue. I feel way behind my friends."

As she shared her story, she described how she had given five years of her twenties to setting up adoption services in China, which she loved doing. When she returned home, though, it seemed as if she had lost her way—or so she felt. And of course, it was all her fault.

"There's no man in my life," she continued. "No golden door has opened to the great career. I've had four dead-end jobs in five years. It's taken all this time for me to find a path I really want to pursue. I feel like such a failure."

I sensed as we talked just how shaken her confidence really was—and how distant God seemed to her. "How are you going to look at what you're calling 'the wasted years'? I mean, where has God been in all that?" I asked.

God had mostly been waiting for her to get her act together, she replied, and we both laughed.

"But God could have shown you what you needed to see a month after you left China, and he didn't," I reminded her. "How are you going to let that mean something in your life?"

This is truly the crucial question for each of us. How am I going to allow the detours and the lost years and the mistakes to take their proper place in a life that is, somehow, being orchestrated by a God who loves me? Can I let myself accept that I am living a directed life even when I feel that I am floundering?

Perhaps my friend's struggle to find her way is not a pile of wasted years in the real scheme of things. I think that is much closer to the truth. I suspect she will come to see that those years contained tiny seeds that blossomed in ways she can hardly imagine now. There is an old expression that comforts because it's just so true: God never wastes an experience on us. If we have given ourselves to him in any true measure, we find it all serves. All of it.

Perhaps you know how awkward it feels, sometimes, when you meet someone for the first time and about ten minutes into the conversation, the question appears: "So what do you do?" Depending on the season of your life, you fish around for some way to explain what you currently *do*. Surely there is some label that makes sense— some tag that describes the way you spend your days.

At many points in my life, I've found that a hard question. A woman's life has always seemed more complicated than a couple of neat labels can explain adequately. But I've noticed that as I've traveled farther in this journey with God, my own focus has changed shape. It matters less what I do out there in the world. The real question becomes more like *what am I meant to give?*

I am grateful for the women I've known through the years. Some wear real pearls and travel to exotic places. And others have hardly left the place where they were born. But the common theme that emerges from the lives of women who smile at the future—women who love their lives—is that they've discovered the intersection where their deep gladness and the world's deep hunger meet.

A sense of purpose is meant to govern our lives. The apostle Paul said that he was always moving forward, pressing on, longing to "lay hold of that for which . . . [he] was laid hold of by Christ Jesus" (Phil. 3:12 NASB). We want to lay hold of the reason God laid hold of us—because there is a reason.

What I'm really saying is that the work of our hands and hearts, offered in his name, makes a difference. God takes what seems common and makes it extraordinary in his kingdom. We may live in a grand house on a hill—or be the daughter of a sharecropper. But our journey is really about finding this work in one form or another. You will know it when you do. It may not look momentous to anyone else, but you know it's right because there's joy there. Or as Madeleine L'Engle writes in one of her poems:

To grow up
is to find
the small part you are playing
in this extraordinary drama
written by
somebody else.[1]

It is a small part you and I are called to play—but it's a small part in an incredible drama. And growing up is somehow about the courage to claim our part.

The fine irony is this: discovering that small part, the one with your name on it, is often the phoenix that rises from the ashes of your broken dreams. This truth caught me by surprise. We think of offering God our talents, but he is not in short supply. He is not all that impressed with our talent.

Rather, what God gives you to give the world often comes from your wounds and secret griefs. As with the friend of mine who counseled women considering abortion, these past griefs can become the passion that fuels your heart. They are the places where you hear God's voice. In some mysterious way, God redeems what's been lost and then transforms it into the cup of cold water you offer in his name. And that is, truly, better than your original dreams of the life you thought you wanted.

As I write this, I see the faces of women who've lived this reality. There's Marge, a fabric artist whose creations speak of the beauty and wholeness she discovered on the far side of debilitating depression. Or Debra, whose father died before she knew him. Her great joy is sponsoring a forgiveness ministry for prison inmates whose children get to visit them for the day. I think of Diana, who opened her home to Russian orphans after her husband's bike accident. Truly, some of the richest pleasures in life come from the gifts you give out of the understanding and empathy that pain has brought you.

Women who emerge from the pages of Scripture also speak of how God redeems and transforms broken dreams into good gifts. If we had known Rahab, whose name is always followed by her ignominy—Rahab, the harlot—would anyone have guessed that her courageous act of trusting the God of Israel for deliverance would take her from an empty existence as a prostitute . . . to a life of wife and mother (see Josh. 2:1–24; Matt. 1:1–17)? Yet her son Boaz can be held up as the Old Testament paragon of a truly righteous man.

When I talk with a woman who can't see light in the tunnel of her life, I often ask her, "What brings you joy? What do you do that makes you secretly glad you were put on the planet for moments like this?" And when she responds that her life is so full of duty and obligation that she has stopped thinking in terms of what she enjoys, I know we are in trouble. When a woman gets weighed down with responsibilities, when hard things have happened . . . there's a great temptation to let go of the joy part. We stop looking for what we are put here to offer.

This is not the way Christ lived. Scripture makes clear that his hands were clasped around the nails that pinned him to a cross of suffering, but his eyes were focused on the joy.

> Fixing our eyes on Jesus, the author and perfecter of faith, who for the joy set before Him endured the cross, despising the shame . . . (Heb. 12:2 NASB)

Christ's joy was the redemption that would come from his great sacrifice. His life was not about *have to, ought to, should*—suffering for the sake of suffering. Christ's great pleasure was that he would bring us home to the Father.

That principle translates by small measures into our lives as well. For there is no joy quite like that of offering what you sense you are meant to give—whether that's creating beautiful table settings for a meeting or counseling women in distress or teaching a Bible study or having a hospitable home. Or like my friend who fixes two dozen biscuits twice a day for children who need a mother. To simply walk out a journey with Christ and give out of whatever grief has been yours is to taste real joy.

The Larger Story God Is Writing with Your Life
Paula Rinehart (*Better Than My Dreams*)

Years ago, I came upon the words of Jim Elliot, a missionary killed by Auca Indians in Ecuador to whom he brought the gospel. His death opened the door to the conversion of this remote jungle tribe. In a letter to his wife before his death, he wrote about the experiences they could have enjoyed together—the time they might have spent in each other's company.[2] I have returned to his words many times when I feel the loss of something I had anticipated but which fails to happen—all the what-could-have-beens of life. Elliot writes:

> What is, is actual—what might be simply is not, and I must not therefore query God as though he robbed me—of things that are not. Further, the things that are belong to us, and they are good, God-given and enriched.[3]

There is a quiet release in my spirit (though it can be slow in coming) when I realize that often, my dreams really are not God's dreams. What does not happen was not meant to take place. My failure—or someone else's failure—didn't catch God by surprise, like it slipped under the wire when he wasn't looking. In the words of Job as he spoke to God, "I know that you can do all things; no plan of yours can be thwarted" (Job 42:2 NIV).

There is a bigger drama taking place than you can see through the keyhole now.

Perhaps you had to experience something on the darker side of life to really appreciate the blazing light of Jesus. Maybe you could never have offered true comfort to hurting people if you had not tasted pain so bitter it took your breath away. Perhaps there were flaws in your husband you were meant to miss because there is something more important being worked into both of your hearts than an easy relationship.

I would not for a moment imply that all stories come out neatly packaged. Lots of loose strings in our lives get tied into happier endings past any horizon we can see. God is great, and God is good, as the child's prayer says—but sometimes his greatness and his goodness come together much farther down the road than we would hope.

C. S. Lewis claims that the problem is one of transposition, which is an interesting word he explained this way. Lewis says that the sovereignty and goodness of God is like a symphony that fills the largest concert hall with the most beautiful music imaginable. Only you and I are not in that room. Rather, we are listening to the music through a grainy radio at the kitchen table, trying to follow the melody through the static.[4] That image keeps me sane when I find myself trying to catch, once again, the faint notes of the song God is playing in my life.

God Is Near
Angela Thomas (*A Beautiful Offering*)

My ten-year-old nephew, Simon, took his parents to school for open house. You remember how those go. The classroom is newly decorated. The parents sit in little chairs. And the teacher talks to everyone about assignments, grading, and expectations for the coming year.

In Simon's class the teacher had asked her students to write the answers to a few questions in a notebook for the parents to review. One of the questions was about a wish coming true. Another was about becoming a grown-up. And then there was this question: "Who do you belong to?"

Some of the kids responded with the expected things. "I belong to my parents" or "I belong to a family" or "I belong to the Boy Scouts."

Simon wrote, "I belong to heaven."

His answer takes my breath away and makes me cry at the same time. My little soccer-star nephew knows where he belongs. Wow. I love that so much.

When I was ten, I didn't know for sure that I belonged to heaven. I was afraid that one wrong move could keep me out. Can you imagine what a difference it will make in Simon's life because that truth is already settled in his soul—he belongs to heaven? Jesus said that when we have called him our Savior, then we belong to heaven too. It's our home, the kingdom of our citizenship, the place our hearts long to be.

When I think of my secret life with God, I picture myself in his arms, comforted by his merciful forgiveness, strengthened by his words of encouragement, and close enough to understand his desires for my heart. I imagine myself, a little girl on his lap, being calmed in his presence, laughing and interacting, then sitting quietly in the security of his embrace.

I know this is going to sound girly, but every time I close my eyes and picture myself in the arms of God, I cry. I think I cry because I envision the arms of God protecting me, and I am relieved to remember his strength when I am weak. When I close my eyes, I see that I really do belong to him. No matter what comes to me or doesn't, I still belong to the Lord God Almighty, the King of heaven and earth.

Maybe I cry because sometimes I'm afraid to be all grown-up and alone, but in my secret place with God, I remember that I am never alone.

In the secret place we can bury ourselves in the robes of God. We can be renewed and strengthened by the covering of his glory. We can hide underneath the shadow of his wings until we are healed and secure in his love. God rewards the secret life with a God-confidence. The woman who maintains this intimacy with her Father learns to interact with the world from the security of her relationship with God.

In the secret place, God whispers until we remember, "You belong to heaven. No one else can have you. No enemy can overtake you. No temptation will overcome you. No disease will destroy you. It is sure. It has been decided. You belong to me."

Notes

INTRODUCTION: FINDING OUR WAY AGAIN

1. Retold from a story in Ken Gire, *Windows of the Soul* (Grand Rapids, MI: Zondervan, 1996), 215.
2. Henri J. M. Nouwen, *The Return of the Prodigal Son* (New York: Image Books, Doubleday, 1994), 82.

1: HIDING IN GUILT AND SHAME

1. Lewis Smedes, *Shame and Grace: Healing the Shame We Don't Deserve* (New York: HarperOne, 1994), 3.
2. John Ortberg, *The Life You've Always Wanted* (Grand Rapids, MI: Zondervan, 2002), 137.
3. James G. Friesen et al., *The Life Model: Living from the Heart Jesus Gave You* (Van Nuys: Shepherd's House, 2000), 8.

2: HOLDING ON TO OUR BROKEN DREAMS

1. J. B. Phillips, *Your God Is Too Small: A Guide for Believers and Skeptics Alike* (Carmichael, CA: Touchstone, 1997), n.p.
2. Ibid.

3. *Chariots of Fire* ©1981. Enigma Productions, Goldcrest Film Ltd., Warner Bros.

4: STRUGGLING WITH DOUBT AND FEAR
1. A.W. Tozer, *The Pursuit of God* (Create Space ed., 2009) 48.

5: FEELING AS IF WE'LL NEVER MEASURE UP
1. Ilene Lelchuk, "Girls Reporting High Stress Over Looks, Weight," *San Francisco Chronicle*, 29 October 2006.

8: STUDYING THE BIBLE
1. Karl Bernhard Garve (1763-1841), Lutheran minister and hymn writer.

9: LEARNING TO BE AUTHENTIC
1. Brennan Manning, "Living as God's Beloved," in *Discipleship Journal*, Issue 100, July/August 1997.
2. David Stewart, *Southern California Cold Waters* (Santa Ana, CA), n.p.
3. Frederick Buechner, *Wishful Thinking: A Theological ABC* (New York: Harper & Row, 1973), 95.
4. Brennan Manning, *Abba's Child* (Colorado Springs: NavPress, 1994), 164.

12: REMEMBERING YOU ARE CHOSEN
1. Madeleine L'Engle, *The Ordering of Love* (Colorado Springs: Crosswicks, Ltd., 2005), 55. Used by permission of Waterbrook Press. All rights reserved.
2. Elisabeth Elliot, *Shadow of the Almighty: The Life and Testament of Jim Elliott* (San Francisco: HarperSanFrancisco, 1989), 160.

3. Ibid.

4. C. S. Lewis, "Transposition," in *The Weight of Glory* (New York: Macmillan, 1949), 55.

About the Authors

JILL BRISCOE currently serves as minister-at-large for Elmbrook Church in Brookfield, Wisconsin, with her husband, Stuart, who served there as senior pastor for thirty years. In addition to her extensive writing and international speaking ministry, she also advises numerous nonprofit organizations and has served on the boards of World Relief and Christianity Today, Inc. Jill and Stuart have three children and thirteen grandchildren.

DR. JILL HUBBARD is a clinical psychologist and regular cohost on Christian radio's nationally syndicated *New Life Live* program. Dr. Jill has gained a reputation for her gentle and insightful style of connecting with radio callers. As the program's only female cohost, she lends a woman's perspective to addressing callers' psychological and spiritual concerns. She is also in private practice where she sees clients who struggle with depression, addictions, eating disorders, and relational and personal growth issues. Dr. Jill lives with her family in southern California.

TAMMY MALTBY is cohost of the four-time Emmy-nominated TV talk show *Aspiring Women* on the Total Living Network. She reaches thousands of women each year through her speaking ministry and has been featured on *The 700 Club*, *Focus on the Family*, *Family Life Today* with Dennis Rainey, *Life Today* with James Robison, and *Midday Connection* as well as hundreds of other radio and television programs.

MARILYN MEBERG speaks each year to 350,000 women at the Women of Faith conferences and is the author of several books. Never one to avoid the hard questions of life, Marilyn Meberg shares the wisdom she's gained from two master's degrees and a private counseling practice.

 STORMIE OMARTIAN is the best-selling author of *The Power of Praying* series with over thirteen million copies sold. In high demand as an international speaker, Stormie's passion is to help people know God and his love in a deep way. A survivor of child abuse, Stormie brings a deep understanding of recovery issues to her work. She and her husband, Michael, have been married for thirty-two years and have three grown children.

 PAULA RINEHART has touched women's lives through writing, speaking, and ministry for more than twenty years. She is the author of the widely acclaimed book *Strong Women, Soft Hearts* and a more recent work, *What's He Really Thinking?* Paula also maintains a private counseling practice in Raleigh, North Carolina. She and her husband, Stacy, have two grown children.

 ANGELA THOMAS is an ordinary woman and mom with an extraordinary passion for God. She's been honored to walk alongside women of all ages and walks of life through her books and speaking engagements. Angela received her master's degree from Dallas Theological Seminary. For more information on Angela, visit: www.angelathomas.com.

SHEILA WALSH has spoken to over four million women at Women of Faith conferences around the country. She is the author of the award-winning *Gigi, God's Little Princess* series and the book and Bible study *Beautiful Things Happen When a Woman Trusts God*. Soon to be released is her new fiction trilogy, *Angel Song*. Sheila lives in Frisco, Texas, with her husband, Barry, and son, Christian.

LISA WHITTLE is the visionary implementer of various women's ministries and events, as well as the coordinator of the Proverbs 31 She Seeks ministry to twenty-somethings. Through insightful Bible teaching, and with a refreshingly authentic faith, Lisa challenges women to develop a more vibrant relationship with Jesus Christ. A graduate of Liberty University, Lisa has done master's work in marriage and family counseling at Southwestern Baptist Theological Seminary. She has authored several books including *Behind Those Eyes: What's Really Going on Inside the Souls of Women* and *The 7 Hardest Things God Asks a Woman to Do*. She has been a featured contributor in the *Women of Faith Connections* magazine, and she is currently working on her third book project. Lisa and her husband, Scott, live with their three children just outside Charlotte, where they laugh a lot and try to live a very real life.

new from WOMEN of FAITH

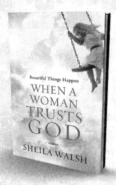

BEAUTIFUL THINGS HAPPEN WHEN A WOMAN TRUSTS GOD

By Sheila Walsh, wherever books are sold

In a message rooted in hope and substantial Bible teaching, Sheila Walsh helps women to see the beautiful things that can happen in their own lives and in the lives of those they love when they fully trust their heavenly Father during good and bad times.

NOTHING IS IMPOSSIBLE

Wherever books are sold

In this Women of Faith devotional, women will encounter page after page of encouragement, humor, insight, and teaching to rediscover the God who will not let them go.

KALEIDOSCOPE

By Patsy Clairmont

Acclaimed author and Women of Faith speaker Patsy Clairmont causes women's hearts to leap and their hopes to lift in this quirky, straight-to-the-point look at the Proverbs.

TELL ME EVERYTHING

By Marilyn Meberg, available 3/30/2010

With the wisdom of a counselor and the whit of a comedian, Marilyn Meberg untangles the issues in women's lives that hold them back from a vibrant relationship with Christ.

FRIENDSHIP FOR GROWN-UPS

By Lisa Whelchel, available 5/4/2010

Former *Facts of Life* star Lisa Whelchel shares her experiences of growing up without true friends, how she learned to find and develop them as an adult through God's grace, and how readers should actively pursue meaningful friendships as adults.

DOING LIFE DIFFERENTLY

By Luci Swindoll, available 5/4/2010

An inspiring account of Luci Swindoll's courageous life that teaches readers how to live savoring each moment, how to let go of regrets, and how to embrace dreams.

THOMAS NELSON

Since 1798